THE
NATION'S
FAVOURITE
HEALTHY
FOOD

NEVEN MAGUIRE

THE
NATION'S
FAVOURITE
HEALTHY
FOOD

GILL & MACMILLAN

Gill & Macmillan

Hume Avenue

Park West

Dublin 12

www.gillmacmillanbooks.ie

© Neven Maguire 2015

978 07171 6799 9

Compiled by Orla Broderick

Edited by Kristin Jensen

Designed by www.grahamthew.com

Photography and prop styling © Joanne Murphy (www.joanne-murphy.com)

Photography assistants: Clare Wilkinson and Ross Murphy Cooke

Food styling by Karen Convery

Indexed by Eileen O'Neill

Printed by L.E.G.O SpA

PROPS

Avoca: Kilmacanogue Store, Cafés & HQ, Wicklow; www.avoca.ie

Meadows and Byrne: The Pavilion, Royal Marine Road,
Dún Laoghaire, Co. Dublin; (01) 280 4554;
www.meadowsandbyrne.com

Considered by Helen James exclusively for Dunnes Stores: Dunnes Stores,
Cornelscourt, Bray Road, Foxrock, Dublin 18; (01) 289 2677

Two Wooden Horses: Delgany, Co. Wicklow;
www.twowoodenhorses.com

This book is typeset in 10 on 12pt Neutra Text Book.

The paper used in this book comes from the wood pulp of managed forests. For
every tree felled, at least one tree is planted, thereby renewing natural resources.

A CIP catalogue record for this book is available from the British Library.

5 4 3 2 1

DEDICATION

This book is dedicated to my wonderful and very special wife, Amelda, who has given me a lot of inspiration and support. I know you are really going to enjoy this book. Thank you and I love you.

ACKNOWLEDGEMENTS

This book simply could not have happened without my long-term collaborator and dear friend, Orla Broderick. You always add so much to the book.

Thanks to Karen Convery who has worked on many of my television shows. This is her first cookbook – take a bow, well done! Thanks also to Olivia Rafftery, Claire Beasley, Pamela Doherty, Clare Wilkinson, Ross Murphy Cooke and, of course, Amelda for all their work testing the recipes – and who got well-fed too!

Thanks to Graham Thew for another brilliant design job and to Joanne Murphy for her wonderful photography. I'm so pleased with the outcome. Thanks also to Kristin Jensen for her excellent editing skills.

A special thank you to my hard-working and very loyal head chef Glen Wheeler and sous chef Carmel McGirr, who organised all of the food for the photography and recipe testing. Your help is very much appreciated.

Thanks as usual to the 'A-Team' at Gill & Macmillan, especially to Nicki Howard for her insight, passion and dedication – I always enjoy working with you. Thanks to Catherine Gough and Teresa Daly for another job well done, and thank you to Michael Gill for his personal interest.

RTÉ has played a huge part in my career. It began when John Masterson, my agent, believed in me and gave me my first break on *Open House* in 1998 – I can't thank him enough for that and for his friendship and support. Thank you to Brian Walsh for his continued support – I admire his passion for food. To David Hare, who produces my TV shows, thank you for always showing my best side – you are a true gent to work with. Thanks also to Billy Keady and Ray de Brún.

A huge thanks to my friends Marty Whelan, Mary Kennedy and Marian Finucane, who have always supported me from day one. I'm forever grateful.

Thank you to Purcell Masterson for advice and support over the years and thanks particularly to Mary Tallent and the whole Purcell Masterson team.

Thanks also to Colm Bradley from Hype & Holler for all your innovative ideas and great work on social media.

A big thank you to Bord Bia for their continued support, especially Aidan Cotter and Theresa Brophy. A huge thank you also to Hylda Adams, who has been a great mentor to me throughout my career. I can't thank you enough.

Thanks to Mairead Lavery, David Leydon, Joe Lenehan and the whole *Irish Farmers Journal* team. I really enjoy writing for you every week.

Thank you to all the media of which there are too many to mention – the list would go on and on! Thank you so much for all of your support and loyalty throughout my career.

Thank you to Eoin O'Flynn at Flogas for his continued support and friendship, and to Kenneth Maguire. To Andrea Doherty, who's like a guardian angel, for managing my diary and organising all my demos. I'm lucky to have you as part of my team.

To my team at the restaurant, who I consider part of the family, a big thanks for all of your hard work and loyalty. You are what makes the MacNean Restaurant a success. A particular thanks to Kevin Ashley, whose love and passion for growing all of our salads, herbs and vegetables is infectious.

Thank you to all my supporters and the people I meet all over the country. You provide such inspiration and give me great feedback about my recipes. I hope you will enjoy this book as much as my others and that it gives you a lot of inspiration to enjoy healthy and delicious food.

Finally, I feel very lucky and privileged to have come from a very close family. Thank you for all of your love and support, especially Amelda, Connor and Lucia. I hope you enjoy this book.

Neven

CONTENTS

INTRODUCTION | IX

JUICES

Carrot, Ginger, Mint and Orange Juice **2**

Beetroot, Orange, Apple and Pear Juice **5**

Avocado, Cucumber, Spinach, Kale, Pineapple and Coconut Juice **6**

Fennel, Blueberry, Apple and Lemon Juice **9**

Celery, Pear, Apple and Ginger Juice **10**

SOUPS

Chicken, Shiitake and Cannellini Bean Soup **15**

Chicken and Coconut Soup **16**

Minestrone Soup with Pesto **18**

Butter Bean and Bacon Soup **21**

Root Vegetable, Chicken and Orzo Soup **22**

SAINTLY SNACKS

Tuna and Hummus Bruschetta **26**

Red Pepper and Chilli Hummus with Crispy Tortilla Chips **29**

Nutty Energy Bites **30**

Kale Crisps **33**

Spice-Crusted Butternut Squash Wedges with Tahini Sauce **34**

LOW-CARB LUNCHES

Tricolour Quinoa, Mediterranean Vegetable and Mozzarella Salad **38**

Tabbouleh Salad with Pomegranate and Goat's Cheese **41**

Roasted Red Pepper and Walnut Dip with Crudités **43**

Crunchy Vietnamese Chicken Salad **44**

Fragrant Duck Salad **47**

LUNCHBOXES

Wraps **51**

Open Sandwiches **53**

Crispbreads **54**

Lettuce Cups **57**

Pitta Breads **58**

SALADS

Pear, Blue Cheese and Spinach Salad with Walnuts **63**

Roasted Beetroot, Feta and Watercress Salad **64**

Warm Spicy Tiger Prawn Salad **66**

Crab, Avocado and Mango Salad **68**

Three Tomato and Beetroot Salad with Harissa and Goat's Cheese **71**

FISH

Fresh Tuna Niçoise **74**

Miso Grilled Hake with Avocado and Lime Salsa **76**

Spicy Prawn Cakes with Ginger **78**

Sea Bass with Ginger and Chilli **81**

Grilled Sardines with Salsa Verde **83**

CHICKEN

Garlic and Lemon Chicken with Rocket **86**

Chicken Kiev with Sweet Potato Chips **88**

Chicken Tabbouleh Salad with Tahini Drizzle **91**

Cashew Nut Chicken and Asparagus Salad with Mango Salsa **92**

Baked Chicken and Chorizo Rice with Artichokes **95**

PORK

Orange and Thyme Pork Steaks with Winter Slaw **99**

Pork Goulash with Cauliflower Rice **100**

Parma-Wrapped Pork Fillet with Pesto and Stir-Fried Curly Kale **102**

Spanish Meatball and Butter Bean Stew **104**

Chinese Pork and Three Pepper Stir-Fry **107**

BEEF

Beef Kofta Curry **110**

Vietnamese Beef Noodle Soup (Pho Bo) **112**

Minute Steaks with White Bean Purée and Sautéed Savoy Cabbage **114**

Roast Rolled Rib of Beef with Horseradish Crème Fraîche **116**

Chargrilled Thai Beef Salad **118**

LAMB

One Tray Greek Lamb Mezze **123**

Lamb Fillet with Blue Cheese and Mint Dressing **125**

Moroccan Spiced Lamb Koftas with Chunky Salad and Pitta **126**

Seared Lamb Fillet with Mediterranean Butter Bean Stew **128**

Chargrilled Lamb Chops with Lemon and Herb Quinoa **131**

VEGETARIAN

Roasted Aubergines with Cherry Tomatoes and Goat's Cheese **134**

Porcini and Artichoke Pasta **137**

Crispy Spinach and Feta Filo Pie **138**

Spicy Roasted Root Vegetables with Lemon and Herb Couscous **141**

Griddled Halloumi with Red Onion, Haricot Bean and Tomato Salad **143**

EGGS

Egg and Cauliflower Curry **146**

Smoked Haddock Hash with Poached Eggs **148**

Irish Breakfast Omelette **151**

Pancetta Baked Eggs **153**

Smoked Salmon and Watercress Crêpes **154**

TAKEAWAY MY WAY

Seafood Paella **159**

Baked Fish and Chips **160**

Peppered Beef Burgers with Sweet Potato Wedges **162**

Pad Thai Stir-Fried Noodles with Pork **164**

Pulled Chicken with Crispy Tacos **167**

OMEGA-3

Cauliflower and Hazelnut Salad **171**

Smoked Trout and Prawn Salad with Avocado and Tomato Salsa **173**

Brown Soda Scones with Walnuts and Flaxseeds **174**

Spaghetti with Sardines **177**

Crispy Salmon with Pomegranate and Watercress Couscous **178**

WHEAT FREE

Fragrant Pork and Sweet Potato Thai Red Curry **183**

Mackerel with Braised Puy Lentils and Sherry Vinaigrette **184**

Cumin Roasted Lamb with Pumpkin Mash **187**

Warm Steak Salad with Horseradish Mustard and Balsamic Vinegar **188**

Tomato and Red Pepper Broth with Borlotti Beans and Cavolo Nero **190**

DAIRY FREE

Spicy Chicken Noodles with Mango **194**

Griddled Salmon with Avocado and Sun-Dried Tomatoes **196**

Garlic and Mustard Beef Skewers with Creamy Chive Drizzle **199**

Satay Prawn Sticks with Griddled Limes **200**

Rosemary Roast Lamb Chops with Roasted Potatoes and Cherry Tomatoes **203**

REFINED SUGAR FREE

Coconut Carrot Slices **207**

Cinnamon French Toast with Berries and Lime Crème Fraîche **208**

Coconut, Mango and Lemon Rice Pudding **210**

Hotcakes with Mango and Banana Sauté **212**

Apple and Pecan Muffins **215**

KIDS' FAVOURITES

Fresh Fruit Ice Lollies **218**

Peanut Butter and Banana French Toast Sandwiches **221**

Quick Quesadillas with Cherry Tomato and Avocado Salsa **223**

Crispy Chicken Strips with Peanut Satay Sauce **224**

Healthy Anzac Biscuits **226**

DESSERTS

Caramel Pear Tart **230**

Sticky Orange Upside Down Cake **233**

Coffee Cake with Mixed Toffee Nuts **234**

Crème Pots with Seasonal Berries **237**

Spiced Poached Pears with Crème Fraîche and Toasted Almonds **238**

INDEX | 241

INTRODUCTION

I love meeting people all over the country at my cookery demonstrations, and teaching and entertaining people from all walks of life at my cookery school and restaurant in Blacklion. It keeps me in touch with how the nation is eating, and one thing I'm hearing loud and clear these days is ... you want to be HEALTHY!

I've found that there is no 'one size fits all' when it comes to healthy eating. What's good for one person isn't necessarily good for another, so I've had to make sure I adapt and cater for all of my customers, whether they are coeliac, have an intolerance, are looking for low-carb options, or want something a little bit naughty but guilt-free!

Most of all, as a chef, it is crucial that the food tastes great; you're not going to eat healthily long term if you aren't enjoying your food. Having devised, tested and tasted each and every one of these recipes, I can assure you they all taste fantastic.

Since having my twins and seeing the amazing reaction to my *Complete Baby & Toddler Cookbook*, my eyes have been opened to how important it is to instill a love of good, healthy and nutritious food in our children – and children learn by watching grown-ups!

Just one or two changes to our eating habits can make a big difference, so join me in a modern way of eating by putting healthier choices on our kitchen tables so we can all feel better together.

healthy

Happy cooking!

Neven

JUICES

Carrot, Ginger, Mint and Orange Juice

Sharp, crisp green apples such as Granny Smiths are perfect for using in juices, as are Braeburn, Egremont or Discovery, which are all normally blushed with red. Apples make a fantastic base juice and are laden with healthy properties from their vitamin, mineral, malic acid and fibre content. They are not only detoxifying, but can also help lower cholesterol, aid digestion and improve the condition of the skin.

4 large carrots, topped and tailed

2 oranges, peeled and separated into quarters

2 green apples, cored and cut into quarters

2.5cm (1in) piece of fresh root ginger, peeled

6 fresh mint sprigs

large handful of ice cubes

MAKES 750ML (1 ¼ PINTS)

Juice each of the ingredients and pour into a jug. Give the juice a quick stir before pouring into glasses half-filled with ice cubes and serve immediately.

Beetroot, Orange, Apple and Pear Juice

Beetroot juice has a distinctly earthy taste that gives a hint of its rich mineral and vitamin content. As such, beetroots are one of the most cleansing, blood-boosting, tonic-like juices there is. Here I've put them with plenty of sweet fruits, which makes this juice all the more palatable.

2 medium beetroots, topped and tailed and then cut into halves or quarters, depending on their size

2 crisp apples, cored and cut into quarters

2 oranges, peeled and separated into quarters

1 pear, cored and cut into quarters

2.5cm (1in) piece of fresh root ginger, peeled

large handful of ice cubes

MAKES 750ML (1 ¼ PINTS)

Juice each of the ingredients and pour into a jug. Give the juice a quick stir before pouring into glasses half-filled with ice cubes and serve immediately.

Avocado, Cucumber, Spinach, Kale, Pineapple and Coconut Juice

One of the most refreshing, tangy combinations there is. Kale is one of nature's wonder foods, as it is loaded with vitamins (especially A and C) and minerals. As such, it is very cleansing, immune-boosting, skin-healing and bone-building and is generally an excellent all-rounder. However, its taste isn't for everyone, which is why adding the pineapple, lime and coconut makes this juice more delicious.

1 ripe avocado, peeled and stone removed

1 small pineapple, peeled, quartered and tough stalk removed

½ cucumber

large handful of baby spinach leaves

handful of kale

300ml (½ pint) coconut water

juice of 1 lime

handful of ice cubes

MAKES 750ML (1 ¼ PINTS)

Juice the avocado, pineapple, cucumber, spinach and kale and pour into a jug, then add the coconut water and lime juice. Give the juice a quick stir before pouring into glasses half-filled with ice cubes to serve.

Fennel, Blueberry, Apple and Lemon Juice

This juice has a tangy, liquorice-like taste from the fennel. The apples and blueberries add a fantastic sweetness laden with antioxidants.

2 small fennel bulbs, topped and tailed and then cut into quarters

2 apples, cored and cut into quarters

200g (7oz) blueberries

juice of 2 lemons

large handful of ice cubes

MAKES 750ML (1 ¼ PINTS)

Put the fennel, apples and blueberries through a juicer, then pour into a jug. Stir in the lemon juice and pour into a glass half-filled with ice cubes to serve.

Celery, Pear, Apple and Ginger Juice

This juice uses two of my favourite fruits combined with refreshing celery, which adds an almost salty quality to the juice, and a tangy hint of ginger. Celery is a cleansing, soothing juice with diuretic properties that help to rid the body of excess water.

6 celery stalks, trimmed

4 small pears, cored and quartered

2 crisp red apples, cored and quartered

5cm (2in) piece of fresh root ginger, peeled

juice of 2 lemons

large handful of ice cubes

MAKES 750ML (1 ¼ PINTS)

Press the celery, pears, apples and ginger through your juicer and pour into a jug. Stir in the lemon juice and then pour into glasses half-filled with ice cubes to serve.

Chicken, Shiitake and Cannellini Bean Soup

This is an incredibly healthy soup that uses no oil but is packed full of flavour. Palm sugar is made from the sap of the *Arenga pinnata* (sugar palm) and the nipa palm. It's now becoming more widely available outside of ethnic supermarkets, but can happily be replaced with coconut sugar, which is produced in an identical way but obviously from a different species.

25g (1oz) dried shiitake mushrooms

2 tbsp cornflour

1.2 litres (2 pints) chicken stock

4 skinless, boneless chicken thighs, diced

2.5cm (1in) piece of fresh root ginger, peeled and thinly sliced

1 tsp harissa paste

1 x 400g (14oz) can of cannellini beans, drained and rinsed

2 tbsp soy sauce

2 tsp palm sugar

sea salt and freshly ground black pepper

fresh coriander leaves, to garnish

griddled sourdough bread, to serve

SERVES 4–6

Soak the mushrooms in boiling water for 20 minutes. Use a bowl so that the mushrooms get completely submerged in the water.

Meanwhile, mix the cornflour in a small bowl with a little water to form a smooth paste. Set aside until needed.

When the mushrooms have softened, drain through a fine sieve and reserve the soaking liquid, then thinly slice the mushrooms. Pour the chicken stock into a large pan and add the sliced mushrooms, diced chicken, ginger and harissa paste. Bring to the boil, then reduce the heat and simmer for 20 minutes.

Pour in the reserved mushroom soaking liquid and then stir in the cornflour mixture, cannellini beans, soy sauce and palm sugar. Bring back to a simmer and season to taste. Cook for another minute or two, stirring until the cornflour has slightly thickened the soup.

Ladle into warmed bowls and garnish with the coriander leaves. Place the griddled bread on the side to serve.

Chicken and Coconut Soup

A wonderfully fragrant soup that always transports me back to Thailand.
Of course, you could replace the chicken with prawns if you prefer or even use a
mixture of both, which is quite traditional in Asian cookery.

2 x 400ml (14fl oz) cans of coconut milk

300ml (½ pint) chicken
or vegetable stock

2.5cm (1in) piece of fresh root ginger,
peeled and thinly sliced

1 lemongrass stalk, halved lengthways

1 tbsp Thai fish sauce (nam pla)

1 tbsp Thai red curry paste

2 x 200g (7oz) skinless chicken
breast fillets

225g (8oz) rice vermicelli noodles

juice of 1 lime

1 mild red chill, seeded and cut
into thin rings
(optional)

fresh coriander sprigs, to garnish

lime wedges, to serve

SERVES 4–6

Place the coconut milk, stock, ginger, lemongrass, Thai fish sauce and red curry paste in a pan. Bring to the boil, whisking to combine, then reduce the heat and simmer for 5 minutes to allow the flavours to develop.

Add the chicken breasts and simmer gently for 8–10 minutes, until cooked through and tender. Transfer the chicken breasts to a plate and leave to cool a little, then shred and set aside until needed. Remove the lemongrass and discard, then quickly blitz the soup with a hand blender for a smooth finish.

Add the noodles and lime juice to the blitzed soup and simmer gently for another 5 minutes, until the noodles are tender.

Using a tongs, divide the noodles among warmed bowls and then ladle over the coconut broth. Top with the shredded chicken and then sprinkle over the red chilli, if using, and coriander sprigs. Serve with a bowl of lime wedges and coriander sprigs.

Minestrone Soup with Pesto

A perfect solution for a cold night: a warming bowl of this chunky Italian soup. If you don't want to add pasta, cooked beans or rice also work well and help to make it a satisfying option, which is actually very healthy and nutritious.

2 tbsp olive oil

1 onion, diced

2 carrots, diced

2 celery sticks, trimmed and diced

1 fennel bulb, trimmed and diced

1 small red chilli, seeded and diced

2 garlic cloves, crushed

2 x 400g (14oz) cans of chopped tomatoes

1.2 litres (2 pints) vegetable stock

1 tbsp tomato purée

150g (5oz) spaghetti, snapped into short lengths

100g (4oz) green beans, trimmed and diced

1 tbsp torn fresh basil

sea salt and freshly ground black pepper

pesto, to garnish (homemade or good-quality shop-bought)

sourdough bread, to serve (optional)

SERVES 6

Heat the olive oil in a large pan over a medium heat. Add the onion, carrots, celery, fennel, chilli and garlic. Sauté for 5 minutes, until softened but not beginning to brown. Stir in the chopped tomatoes, stock and tomato purée. Bring to the boil, then reduce the heat and simmer for 20 minutes, until the liquid has slightly reduced and all the vegetables are completely tender.

Add the spaghetti and simmer for another 10 minutes, until the spaghetti is al dente – tender but still with a little bite.

Stir in the green beans and basil, then season to taste and cook for another minute or two, until the beans are just tender. Ladle into warmed bowls, then add a swirl of pesto to each one. Serve with sourdough bread, if liked.

Butter Bean and Bacon Soup

This soup might sound like an unusual combination of ingredients, but it has a lovely spicy kick that complements the sweetness of the carrots. The addition of a small amount of bacon goes a long way in the flavour stakes and blitzing the butter beans gives a fantastic velvety finish.

1 tbsp rapeseed oil

450g (1lb) carrots, diced

1 onion, diced

50g (2oz) rindless smoked streaky bacon, diced

1 garlic clove, crushed

1 tsp freshly grated root ginger

1 tbsp mild curry powder

1 tsp ground turmeric

1 x 400g (14oz) can of butter beans, drained and rinsed

1.2 litres (2 pints) vegetable stock

200ml (7fl oz) semi-skimmed milk

1 tbsp tomato purée

1 tbsp chopped fresh flat-leaf parsley

sea salt and freshly ground black pepper

SERVES 6

Heat the rapeseed oil in a pan over a medium heat. Sauté the carrots, onion, bacon, garlic and ginger for 10 minutes, until softened and just beginning to catch a little colour. Tip in the curry powder and turmeric and cook for another 2 minutes, stirring.

Stir in the beans, stock, milk and tomato purée. Bring to the boil, then reduce the heat and simmer for 15–20 minutes, until the carrots are completely tender.

Season to taste and stir in the parsley, then remove a ladleful of the chunky ingredients to reserve as a garnish, if liked. Blitz the rest of the soup with a hand blender until smooth. Ladle into warmed bowls and add a spoonful of the reserved ingredients to serve.

Root Vegetable, Chicken and Orzo Soup

Flavourful stock, freshly cooked chicken, root vegetables and noodles make a classic chicken soup. Every country in the world has its own version. I like to use orzo, which is a rice-shaped pasta. Each grain is slightly smaller than a pine nut and is made from hard white semolina. In Italy, orzo is frequently used in soups such as this one.

POACHED CHICKEN:

1.5kg (3 ¼lb) whole chicken

2 celery sticks, chopped

1 large onion, chopped

1 carrot, chopped

2 garlic cloves, sliced

2 bay leaves

2 fresh thyme sprigs

1 tsp black peppercorns

2.5 litres (4 ½ pints) water

SOUP:

2 celery sticks, diced

2 carrots, diced

200g (7oz) orzo pasta (or similar small pasta shapes)

2 fresh thyme sprigs, leaves only

1 tbsp chopped fresh flat-leaf parsley

sea salt and freshly ground black pepper

SERVES 6-8

Place the whole chicken in a large stockpot or pan over a medium heat with the celery, onion, carrot, garlic, bay leaves, thyme, peppercorns and water. Bring to the boil, then cover and reduce the heat to low. Simmer very gently for 1 hour, until the chicken is cooked through. Use a metal spoon to occasionally skim the foam from the surface.

Remove the chicken from the stock and allow it to cool slightly. Strain the stock, discarding the vegetables – you should have 2.5 litres (4 ½ pints) in total. When the chicken is cool enough to handle, remove the skin and shred the meat from the bones, discarding the skin and bones. Set the meat aside.

To finish making the soup, return the stock to a clean pan over a medium heat and add the celery, carrots, orzo pasta and thyme leaves. Bring to the boil, then reduce the heat and simmer for 10 minutes, until the pasta is just tender. Add the cooked shredded chicken, then bring back to a simmer and cook for another 2-3 minutes, until the vegetables are just cooked. Stir in the parsley and season to taste. Ladle into bowls to serve.

SAINTLY SNACKS

Tuna and Hummus Bruschetta

Tuck into this healthy snack to avoid that blood sugar dip and tide yourself over until dinner. This hummus is so easy to make and beats shop-bought every time. Canned tuna is a great option to use, as it's so low in saturated fat. It's also a good source of vitamin B6 and phosphorus and a very good source of protein, niacin, vitamin B12 and selenium.

8 slices of sourdough bread

olive oil, for drizzling

1 garlic clove, cut in half

2 vine-ripened tomatoes, sliced

handful of baby spinach leaves

2 x 120g (4 ¼oz) cans of tuna in spring water, drained

2 tbsp rinsed capers

fresh flat-leaf parsley and basil leaves, to garnish

HUMMUS:

1 x 400g (14oz) can of chickpeas, drained and rinsed

2 garlic cloves, crushed

1 tbsp light tahini (sesame seed paste)

1 tsp ground cumin

1 tsp smoked paprika

5 tbsp water

2 tbsp lemon juice

2 tbsp extra virgin olive oil

sea salt and freshly ground black pepper

SERVES 4

To make the hummus, place the chickpeas in a food processor with the garlic, tahini, cumin and smoked paprika. Blend to a paste. Add the water, lemon juice and olive oil through the feeder tube, then season to taste and blend for a few minutes. Remove from the food processor and place in a suitable container with a lid or cover with cling film. This can be made a few days ahead and stored in the fridge.

Toast the sourdough bread in a toaster or grill under a medium heat until golden. Drizzle each slice with a little olive oil and rub with the cut garlic clove. Spread the bruschetta thickly with the hummus, then arrange the tomato slices on top, followed by the spinach, chunks of tuna and a sprinkling of capers. Divide the bruschetta among plates or use one large platter, then season with pepper and scatter over the parsley and basil to serve.

Red Pepper and Chilli Hummus with Crispy Tortilla Chips

This is a variation on traditional hummus and has a fantastic vibrant colour. Here it gets served with some crispy tortilla chips, which are much lower in fat than the ones that you buy. It would also be great spread on crackers or chunks of warm bread, or scooped up with crispbreads.

1 large red pepper

olive oil, for cooking

1 mild red chilli

1 x 400g (14oz) can of chickpeas, rinsed and drained

juice of 1 lemon

2 garlic cloves, crushed

good pinch of ground cumin

100ml (3 ½fl oz) light tahini (sesame seed paste)

5 tbsp water

extra virgin olive oil, for drizzling

pinch of sweet paprika

sea salt and freshly ground black pepper

lemon wedges, to garnish

CRISPY TORTILLA CHIPS:

4–6 soft multiseed flour tortillas

olive oil, for brushing

SERVES 4–6

Preheat the oven to 200°C (400°F/gas mark 6).

To make the hummus, place the red pepper in a small baking tin and drizzle with a little olive oil. Roast for 20 minutes, then add the chilli and drizzle over a little more olive oil. Continue to cook for another 20–25 minutes, until both vegetables are completely tender and nicely charred. Transfer to a polythene bag and leave to cool completely (this will help to steam the skins off). When cool enough to handle, peel both, then cut in half and remove the cores and seeds. Roughly chop the remaining flesh.

Place the red pepper and chilli flesh in a food processor with the chickpeas, lemon juice, garlic, cumin, tahini and water. Whizz to a creamy purée and season to taste. Transfer to a bowl and smooth the top with the back of a spoon. Drizzle with the extra virgin olive oil and sprinkle over a little sweet paprika and freshly ground black pepper.

To prepare the tortilla chips, place two baking sheets in the oven for about 5 minutes, until they are well heated. Meanwhile, lightly brush both sides of the soft flour tortillas with olive oil, then cut in half. Cut each half into four triangles and arrange on the heated baking sheets. Place in the oven for 3–4 minutes, until crisped up and light gold in colour.

To serve, arrange the crispy tortilla chips on a platter with the bowl of red pepper and chilli hummus. Garnish with lemon wedges.

Nutty Energy Bites

These nutty energy bites have a nice sweetness to them without being overpowering, and a little square or ball will keep you nice and full. I really enjoy them after a workout in the gym, when I feel like I've earned a little treat but don't want to ruin all my hard work. If kept in an airtight container, they keep well for up to two weeks in the fridge.

100g (4oz) flaked or blanched almonds

50g (2oz) Brazil nuts

50g (2oz) cashew nuts

3 tbsp pumpkin seeds

50g (2oz) goji berries, very finely chopped

100g (4oz) desiccated coconut

pinch of sea salt

4 tbsp coconut oil

4 tbsp honey

4 tbsp peanut butter
(no added sugar or salt)

1 tsp vanilla extract

MAKES 25

Place the almonds in a food processor with the Brazil nuts, cashew nuts and pumpkin seeds and pulse until finely chopped. But don't pulse too long – you don't want the nuts to turn to a paste. Tip them into a bowl and stir in the goji berries with half of the desiccated coconut and a pinch of sea salt.

Melt the coconut oil in a pan over a low heat. Once it has melted, remove from the heat and stir in the honey, peanut butter and vanilla extract. Mix well in the pan using a whisk or a fork. Pour this over the nut mixture and stir together until it's all evenly combined. Leave to harden in the fridge for 1–2 hours.

Use a small ice cream scoop to shape the mixture into balls. Sprinkle over the remaining desiccated coconut or roll each ball in it. Place back in the fridge for 2–3 hours to firm up. Serve straight from the fridge.

Kale Crisps

Salty, crispy and addictive, these literally take minutes to prepare and less than 12 minutes to cook. This is a great way to get used to eating kale, even if you think you're not too keen on it. This super-green leaf is a member of the cabbage family and generally comes in two forms: kale, which has smooth leaves, and curly kale, which has crinkly leaves. Curly is the most common of the two.

1 bunch of kale

1 tbsp olive oil

¼ tsp sea salt

SERVES 4

Preheat the oven to 150°C (300°F/gas mark 2). Line two large baking sheets with parchment paper.

Wash the kale and dry it very well. Using a paring knife or kitchen scissors, trim the ribs out of the kale leaves and discard. Cut the remaining kale into pieces, each one roughly 5cm (2in).

Place the kale in a large bowl and drizzle over the olive oil. Toss gently but thoroughly, making sure each piece is well coated.

Arrange on the lined baking sheets in a single layer and sprinkle with the salt. Bake for 8–12 minutes, until just crisp. Start checking after 8 minutes – it's important not to overcook the crisps or they'll burn. I find that some varieties cook faster than others. Remove from the oven and leave to cool for a minute or two, then tip into a bowl and serve immediately.

Spice-Crusted Butternut Squash Wedges with Tahini Sauce

This versatile snack is simple to prepare, but boasts some substantial flavours. It would also work as a starter, vegetarian main course or with a roast leg of lamb or chicken. The tahini sauce is quite dominant, but it's a flavour I've come to really enjoy.

50g (2oz) skinned hazelnuts

2 tbsp sesame seeds

1 tbsp coriander seeds

1 tbsp cumin seeds

1 large butternut squash

1 tbsp olive oil

chopped fresh flat-leaf parsley, to garnish

TAHINI SAUCE:

4 tbsp light tahini (sesame seed paste)

4 tbsp water

2 tsp lemon juice

1 small garlic clove, crushed

sea salt and freshly ground black pepper

SERVES 4

Preheat the oven to 200°C (400°F/gas mark 6).

Place the hazelnuts in a baking tin and toast for 6–8 minutes, until golden. Add the sesame, coriander and cumin seeds and roast for another minute or two. Set aside and leave to cool.

Meanwhile, peel the butternut squash, remove the seeds and slice into long, thin wedges.

When the hazelnut mixture is completely cool, put it into a pestle and mortar with a good pinch of salt and pepper and roughly bash. Place the butternut squash wedges in a large roasting tin and drizzle over the olive oil, tossing to coat. Sprinkle over the spice mixture and spread out the butternut squash wedges in a single layer in the tin. Roast for 30–40 minutes, turning halfway through, until the wedges are cooked through and have started to take on some colour.

Meanwhile, to make the sauce, place the tahini in a small bowl with the water, lemon juice, garlic and a good pinch of salt and some freshly ground black pepper. Whisk until it's the consistency of honey, adding a little more water if necessary.

Spread the spice-crusted butternut squash wedges on a large platter and serve the tahini sauce in a separate bowl. Scatter over the parsley to serve.

LOW-CARB LUNCHES

Tricolour Quinoa, Mediterranean Vegetable and Mozzarella Salad

Quinoa is a gluten-free grain that's rich in essential amino acids and vitamins B2, E and A, plus it contains more iron than any other grain. Tricolour quinoa is a balanced combination of white, black and red quinoa, but of course you can use just one colour if you prefer. They all have the same nutritional value but have different textures, which makes for a more interesting salad.

800ml (1 pint 7fl oz) vegetable stock

300g (11oz) quinoa
(mixture of white, black and red)

1 tbsp olive oil

1 red onion, finely diced

1 small courgette, finely diced

1 roasted red pepper, finely diced
(from a jar or can)

finely grated rind and juice of 1 lemon

2 tbsp chopped fresh flat-leaf parsley

2 x 150g (5oz) buffalo mozzarella balls,
cut or broken into small pieces

100g (4oz) pitted black olives,
cut into quarters

DRESSING:

2 tbsp extra virgin olive oil

1 tbsp balsamic vinegar

½ tsp Dijon mustard

1 garlic clove, crushed

sea salt and
freshly ground black pepper

SERVES 4

Put all the dressing ingredients in a screw-topped jar and season with salt and pepper, then shake until emulsified.

Place the stock in a pan and season to taste, then bring to the boil. Stir in the quinoa and return to the boil. Reduce the heat, then cover and simmer gently for 15 minutes, until soft, or according to the packet instructions. Once the quinoa has cooked, drain it through a sieve and tip into a large bowl. Allow to cool.

Meanwhile, heat the olive oil in a non-stick frying pan over a medium heat. Add the red onion and courgette and sauté for 4–5 minutes, until softened. Remove from the heat and allow to cool a little, then stir in the red pepper. Fold the vegetables into the cooled quinoa with the lemon juice and rind. Stir in the parsley with the dressing and season to taste. Stir in the mozzarella and olives, then divide among bowls to serve.

Tabbouleh Salad with Pomegranate and Goat's Cheese

This is a classic Middle Eastern salad made with cracked wheat, also known as bulghar or burghul wheat. You'll find it in health food shops or alongside the dried pulses and beans in the supermarket. Tabbouleh is traditionally eaten scooped up with small Cos lettuce leaves. These can be arranged on a platter with a separate bowl of the tabbouleh salad alongside.

100g (4oz) bulgur wheat

4 ripe tomatoes, quartered, seeded and diced

large bunch of fresh flat-leaf parsley, leaves stripped and roughly chopped

good handful of fresh mint leaves, roughly chopped

1 bunch of spring onions, trimmed and finely chopped

1 head of Little Gem lettuce

150g (5oz) hard goat's cheese, rind removed and finely diced

1 small pomegranate, halved and seeds taken out (all skin discarded)

DRESSING:

juice of 1 lemon

2 garlic cloves, crushed

pinch of ground cinnamon

good pinch of ground allspice

4 tbsp extra virgin olive oil

sea salt and freshly ground black pepper

SERVES 4

Place the bulgur wheat in a bowl and pour over enough boiling water to cover it. Set aside for 5 minutes, then tip into a sieve and rinse well under cold running water. Drain well and tip into a bowl.

Meanwhile, make the dressing for the tabbouleh. Place the lemon juice in a screw-topped jar with the garlic, cinnamon and allspice. Season to taste and shake until the salt has dissolved. Add the olive oil and shake again until well combined.

Add the diced tomatoes to the drained bulgur wheat with the parsley, mint and spring onions. Stir until well combined. Season with salt and pepper and set aside at room temperature to allow the flavours to develop.

Just before serving, trim down the Little Gem lettuce and separate it into leaves, then tear into small pieces. Give the tabbouleh salad a good stir and gently fold in the lettuce, then scatter over the goat's cheese and pomegranate seeds to serve.

Roasted Red Pepper and Walnut Dip with Crudités

Pomegranate molasses is a fruit syrup made from pomegranate juice. It's a reduction from a tart variety of the fruit, evaporated to form a thick, dark liquid. It has recently become very trendy but has its origins in Iranian and Turkish cuisine. You will find it in good delis and high-end supermarkets, but if unavailable for this recipe, use lemon juice or red wine vinegar instead.

1 tsp cumin seeds

225g (8oz) roasted red peppers, drained (from a jar or can)

100g (4oz) shelled walnut halves

50g (2oz) sun-dried tomatoes in oil, drained

1 garlic clove, chopped

1 tsp smoked paprika

2 tbsp extra virgin olive oil

2 tbsp pomegranate molasses

about 2 tbsp water

sea salt and freshly ground black pepper

selection of crudités, such as raw carrot and cucumber batons, radishes, cauliflower florets and sugar snap peas

SERVES 4

Heat the cumin seeds in a small non-stick frying pan over a medium heat until aromatic. Tip into a pestle and mortar and grind to a fine powder. Put the ground cumin into a food processor with the roasted red peppers, walnuts, sun-dried tomatoes, garlic and smoked paprika. Blend to a rough purée, then pour in the olive oil and pomegranate molasses with enough water to make a smooth dip. Season to taste with salt and pepper.

Using a spatula, transfer the dip to a bowl set on a plate with the crudités.

Crunchy Vietnamese Chicken Salad

This salad is packed full of flavour and has the added bonus of being very transportable. Just keep the dressing in a separate jar and add it right before serving. I love cooking chicken thighs this way, as you end up with crispy skin and succulent flesh.

6 garlic cloves, peeled and sliced

1 large shallot, roughly chopped

1 tbsp minced fresh root ginger

2 tsp maple syrup

4 tbsp dark soy sauce

4 tbsp Thai fish sauce (nam pla)

½ tsp Chinese five-spice powder

8 boneless chicken thighs, with skin

1 tbsp rapeseed oil

100g (4oz) green beans, trimmed and sliced into 2cm (1in) lengths

275g (10oz) mixed baby salad leaves

225g (8oz) cherry plum tomatoes, halved or quartered

1 small red pepper, halved, seeded and diced

1 large carrot, julienned into fine shreds

DRESSING:

juice of 1 lime

2 tbsp extra virgin rapeseed oil

sea salt and freshly ground black pepper

SERVES 4

To make the marinade, place the garlic in a mini blender or pestle and mortar along with the shallot, ginger and maple syrup, then work to a paste. Transfer to a small bowl and whisk in the soy sauce, Thai fish sauce, five-spice powder and several grinds of pepper.

Arrange the chicken thighs in a shallow, non-metallic dish and pour over the marinade, turning until well coated. Cover and chill for at least 2 hours or overnight is best. Bring back to room temperature before cooking and wipe off any excess marinade with kitchen paper. Reserve any remaining marinade.

Heat a large frying pan over a medium heat. Pour in the rapeseed oil, then add the chicken thighs, skin side down. Cook for 20–30 minutes, until the skin is golden and crispy. Don't be tempted to touch them while they are cooking or shake the pan occasionally – just leave them alone and you will produce the most fantastic crisp skin and succulent flesh. If you think that they are starting to catch and burn a little around the edges, add a couple tablespoons of the reserved marinade. When you can see that they are nicely browned and that the flesh is almost but not quite cooked through, turn them over and cook for another 5–6 minutes, until completely cooked through and tender. Remove from the heat and leave to rest in a warm place for 5 minutes.

Plunge the green beans into a pan of boiling salted water for 3–4 minutes, until just tender, then drain and refresh under cold running water.

Place the salad leaves in a large bowl with the blanched beans, tomatoes, red pepper and carrot. Season to taste.

To make the dressing, put the lime juice and oil in a screw-topped jar and season to taste.

To serve, give the dressing a good shake and then use to lightly dress the salad, tossing well to combine. Divide among plates, then carve the chicken thighs into slices and place on top.

Fragrant Duck Salad

I'm a big fan of the authentic Chinese aromatic duck that is readily available in all major supermarkets. It makes this salad quick and easy to prepare. The duck can be cooked a couple of hours ahead of time so that all you have to do is toss all the ingredients together just before you are ready to serve.

1 whole aromatic duck (Silver Hill or similar)

½ head of iceberg lettuce, core discarded and leaves shredded

4 spring onions, trimmed and thinly sliced

1 firm, ripe mango, peeled, stone removed and sliced

1 mild red chilli, halved, seeded and cut into rings

50g (2oz) roasted cashew nuts, roughly chopped

good handful of fresh coriander leaves

DRESSING:

2 tbsp extra virgin rapeseed oil

1 tbsp rice wine vinegar

1 tbsp hoisin sauce

1 tsp finely minced root ginger

few drops of toasted sesame oil

sea salt and freshly ground black pepper

SERVES 4–6

Preheat the oven to 200°C (400°F/gas mark 6).

Remove the packaging from the duck and place the duck on a rack over a roasting tin. Roast for 1 1/2 hours or according to the instructions on the packet, until the skin is crisp and the duck is completely heated through. Remove from the oven and leave to rest for at least 20 minutes, but up to a couple of hours is fine.

Carve the meat from the duck and shred or cut into bite-sized pieces, discarding the bones and skin. Place in a large bowl with the lettuce, spring onions, mango, chilli, cashew nuts and coriander.

To make the dressing, place the oil in a screw-topped jar with the vinegar, hoisin sauce, ginger and sesame oil. Season to taste.

When ready to serve, shake the dressing gently to combine and use to lightly dress the duck salad. Divide among plates and serve straight away.

LUNCHBOXES

Wraps

Take a protein-packed wrap into work or school, when you are travelling or even on a picnic. All these ideas are a feast in a delicious wholemeal wrap or flatbread. If you aren't eating them immediately, it's important to roll them up fairly tightly and wrap them in foil, then chill until ready to eat. Always eat within 24 hours and transport with an ice pack if serving as a packed lunch. Unwrap the foil as you eat the wrap so that everything stays together nicely.

Ham and Egg Salad	Smear a little low-fat mayonnaise down a wholemeal wrap or into the bottom of a split wholemeal pitta bread and arrange a sliced tomato and a few cucumber slices on top. Add a couple of wafer-thin slices of cooked ham and a sliced hard-boiled egg. Finish with a couple of shredded crisp lettuce leaves, then roll up and wrap tightly in tin foil.
Roast Beef with Dijon and Watercress	Smear a little Dijon mustard mixed with crème fraîche down the middle of a wholemeal wrap. Scatter fresh watercress on top and cover with thin slices of roast beef, then season with salt and pepper and add a couple small spoonfuls of hot or sweet pepper jelly. Roll up and wrap tightly in tin foil.
Roasted Red Pepper, Goat's Cheese and Spinach	Spread a wholemeal wrap with a layer of soft goat's cheese and season with salt and pepper. Arrange drained roasted red peppers from a can or jar on top, then scatter over a layer of baby spinach leaves. Roll up and wrap tightly in tin foil.

Open Sandwiches

You can make open sandwiches with just one slice of bread and loads of filling. Experiment with dense pumpernickel-style or rye bread, which has no wheat and therefore has a low GI, but it can take a bit of getting used to. Otherwise, thin slices of brown wheaten bread can be very satisfying, filling you up nicely until your next meal. If you want to take open sandwiches as a packed lunch, try taking all the bits and bobs you need separately and put them together when you're ready to eat.

Chicken Salad with Cress

Lightly smear a little low-fat mayonnaise on two slices of rye bread and top with a sliced tomato and a few cucumber slices. Scatter over a small sliced chicken breast, then season with salt and pepper and snip over a little salad cress.

Mackerel Pâté with Watercress

Skin and flake the flesh of 100g (4oz) smoked mackerel fillets, then mix with 2 tablespoons of natural yoghurt and a dollop of low-fat mayonnaise. Stir in one finely chopped spring onion and a couple of cherry tomatoes that you've cut into quarters. Spread thickly onto two slices of pumpernickel or brown wheaten bread. Top with lots of fresh watercress leaves and season with black pepper. Pack with a lemon wedge.

Smoked Salmon with Horseradish Dressing

Arrange some watercress sprigs and slices of smoked salmon on pumpernickel bread. Drizzle over 1 tablespoon of crème fraîche that has been mixed with 1/2 teaspoon of creamed horseradish and 1/2 teaspoon of Dijon mustard. Season with freshly ground black pepper and pack with a lemon wedge.

Crispbreads

There is now a fantastic range of crispbreads on the market and the selection is growing all the time. Some of my current favourites include quinoa or buckwheat crispbreads, but rice cakes would work well too. It just depends on which ones you like best. Taking your own lunch to work or when you're on the move helps you control what you're eating – just keep an eye on your portion size. Shop-bought sandwiches are often surprisingly high in fat. I often pack a lunchbox with an ice pack in a cool bag with the ingredients I'm going to use, then I put it all together when I'm ready to eat. That way, everything tastes lovely and fresh and looks nice and appetising. Even the guacamole can be made in a matter of minutes – you'll just need to bring along a knife and fork to prepare the avocado.

Guacamole

Cut a firm, ripe avocado in half and scoop out the flesh. Mash the flesh with a fork. Mix in a crushed garlic clove, a squeeze of lime juice, a finely chopped tomato and a few drops of Tabasco and season lightly. Pack into a plastic container with a lid and spread onto the crispbreads. Scatter with fresh coriander leaves to serve.

Parma Ham and Tomatoes

Spread the crispbreads very thinly with low-fat mayonnaise and slices of tomatoes on top. Season with salt and pepper, then arrange a slice of Parma ham on each one. Sprinkle over wild rocket leaves to serve.

Goat's Cheese, Date and Apple

Spread the crispbreads with soft goat's cheese and season with pepper. Scatter over some finely chopped Medjool dates, finely diced celery and some finely diced red-skinned apples tossed with a little lemon juice.

Lettuce Cups

If you're looking for a fresh, crunchy lunchtime experience, then these lettuce cups should fit the bill. As they have no bread they are extremely light, so they won't keep you full for as long. If you're taking them to work or when you're on the move, don't forget to use a cool bag and ice pack to keep everything chilled in separate compartments so that it's all in tip-top condition until you're ready to eat. Bring along some healthy snacks in case you get peckish, such as fresh or dried fruit or small packets of nuts, which seem to be more readily available. I've recently seen them in petrol stations and local shops, so there's really no excuse not to be well stocked up.

Crunchy Thai Turkey Salad

Sauté 1 teaspoon each of freshly grated ginger and garlic in a little rapeseed oil, then stir-fry 100g (4oz) of minced turkey until tender. Stir in a small grated carrot, 40g (1 1/2 oz) finely chopped water chestnuts from a can, 25g (1oz) chopped unsalted roasted peanuts and some chopped fresh coriander. Mix 2 teaspoons each of lime juice and Thai fish sauce (nam pla) with a pinch of palm sugar and use to dress the turkey mixture. Use to fill a Little Gem lettuce that's been separated into leaves and garnish with fresh coriander leaves. Serve with lime wedges.

Cottage Cheese with Tomato and Cucumber Salsa

Mix two chopped tomatoes with half of a cucumber cut into thin slices and four finely chopped spring onions, then season with salt and pepper. Fill a Little Gem lettuce that has been separated into leaves with 4 tablespoons of cottage cheese, then scatter over the tomato and cucumber salsa. Snip some salad cress on top to serve.

Smoked Chicken with Asian Slaw

Lightly dress 200g (7oz) of shredded red cabbage and one small grated carrot with 1 tablespoon of rice wine vinegar and a few drops of toasted sesame oil. Add one or two slices of pickled ginger that you've shredded and a small, thinly sliced smoked chicken breast and mix gently to combine. Use to fill the separated leaves of a Little Gem lettuce.

Pitta Breads

These filled pitta breads combine whole grains, protein, veggies and sometimes a little dairy into one filling meal and only take 5 minutes to make. The best way to avoid making bad food choices is to always have a well-balanced choice to hand.

Prawn, Tomato and Rocket

Mix 10 cooked, peeled prawns with a couple of small, diced tomatoes and tear in a few fresh basil leaves. Dress with a squeeze of lemon juice and a splash of extra virgin olive oil. Season with salt and pepper. Pack into a wholemeal pitta with rocket leaves and snip over some salad cress, then wrap in tin foil until needed.

Ham, Cheese and Pickle

Spread 1 tablespoon of farmhouse pickle or chutney into the bottom of a split wholemeal pitta. Top with 25g (1oz) of grated mature Cheddar and a couple wafer-thin slices of cooked ham. Add a sliced tomato and two thinly sliced dill gherkins. Finish with some fresh watercress, then wrap in tin foil until needed.

Piquant Tuna Salad

Mix 4 tablespoons of 0%-fat Greek yoghurt with 1 teaspoon of Dijon mustard and 1 tablespoon of wholegrain mustard. Season with salt and pepper and add a squeeze of lemon juice and a pinch of cayenne pepper. Fold in a very finely diced celery stick, one finely chopped spring onion and a drained 200g (7oz) can of light tuna chunks in water. Put a handful of leafy greens in the bottom of a split wholemeal pitta and then fill with the tuna mixture. Wrap in tin foil until needed.

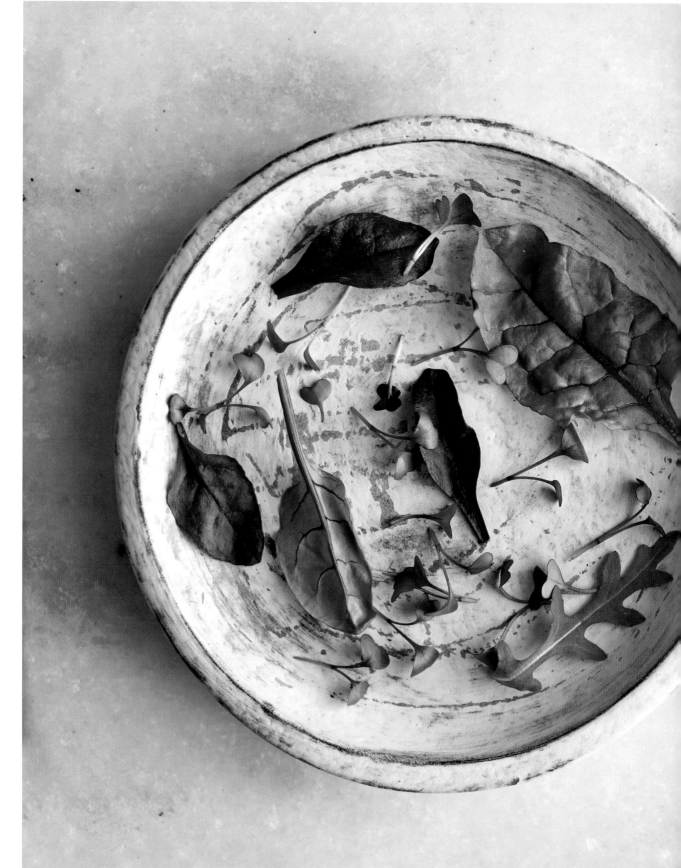

SALADS

Pear, Blue Cheese and Spinach Salad with Walnuts

The sweetness of the pear perfectly contrasts the tanginess of the blue cheese in this simple salad. It makes a great light lunch or starter or could be served with roast pork instead of roast potatoes as a lighter option.

400g (14oz) baby spinach leaves

3 firm, ripe pears

150g (5oz) Cashel Blue or Bellingham Blue cheese

50g (2oz) walnuts, toasted

3 spring onions, thinly sliced

DRESSING:

3 tbsp extra virgin olive oil

1 tbsp red wine vinegar

1 tsp Dijon mustard

1 garlic clove, crushed

sea salt and freshly ground black pepper

SERVES 4-6

For the dressing, put all the ingredients in a screw-topped jar or squeezy bottle and shake until thickened and emulsified. Season to taste and set aside until needed.

Lightly dress the spinach with some of the dressing and arrange on plates or use one large platter. Cut the pears into quarters and remove the cores, then cut into wedges and arrange on top of the spinach.

Lightly crumble over the blue cheese, toasted walnuts and spring onions. Drizzle over the rest of the dressing to serve.

Roasted Beetroot, Feta and Watercress Salad

You could use a jar or vac-pack of cooked baby beetroot, but the ones you roast yourself are so much more delicious and even better a day later, when the flavours have developed. Watercress works so well with beetroot, but you could use rocket or a mixture of leaves from a bag, such as watercress, spinach and rocket.

100g (4oz) watercress

100g (4oz) feta cheese, crumbled

50g (2oz) ready-to-eat dried apricots, finely diced

2 tbsp toasted pine nuts

ROASTED BEETROOT:

500g (1lb 2oz) small raw beetroot, peeled

2 tbsp olive oil

1 tbsp clear honey

2 tsp balsamic vinegar

1 tsp fresh thyme leaves

DRESSING:

1 tbsp sunflower oil

1 tbsp olive oil

1 tbsp good-quality sherry vinegar

1 tsp clear honey

½ small mild red chilli, seeded and finely diced

sea salt and freshly ground black pepper

SERVES 4-6

Preheat the oven to 200°C (400°F/gas mark 6).

Cut each beetroot in half or into quarters until they are all evenly sized. Whisk together the olive oil, honey, balsamic vinegar and thyme, drizzle over the beetroots and season to taste. Toss until all the beetroot is thoroughly coated. Roast for 40–45 minutes, until cooked through and glazed. Leave at room temperature to cool.

Put all the dressing ingredients in a screw-topped jar and season with salt and pepper, then shake until emulsified.

Arrange the watercress on plates or use one large platter. Sprinkle over the cooked baby beetroots, feta, apricots and pine nuts. Just before serving, drizzle over the dressing.

Warm Spicy Tiger Prawn Salad

This salad is absolutely packed full of flavour and uses just 2 teaspoons of toasted sesame oil. Cooked tiger prawns are marinated in a wonderful concoction of Asian ingredients, which almost cook the flesh. They are then flashed in a searing-hot wok just before serving – delicious.

juice of 1 lime

2 tbsp Thai fish sauce (nam pla)

2 tbsp light soy sauce

2 tsp toasted sesame oil

2 tsp palm sugar

2 garlic cloves, crushed

2 lemongrass sticks, trimmed and very finely chopped

1 red chilli, seeded and finely chopped

400g (14oz) cooked tiger prawns, thawed if frozen

1 firm, ripe avocado

1 small, firm, ripe mango

4 spring onions, thinly sliced

2 shallots, thinly sliced

100g (4oz) watercress

SERVES 4–6

Mix the lime juice in a medium-sized bowl with the Thai fish sauce, soy sauce, sesame oil, palm sugar, garlic, lemongrass and red chilli. Add the tiger prawns and mix well to combine, then cover with cling film and leave to marinate in the fridge for 1 hour.

When you are almost ready to serve, cut the avocado in half, take out the stone, peel away the skin and cut the flesh into slices. Do the same with the mango.

Heat a wok until it's smoking hot. Toss the spring onions and shallots into the marinating prawns, then tip the whole lot into the wok. Stir-fry for 2–3 minutes, until just heated through. Be careful not to overcook.

Arrange the watercress on plates or use one large platter. Divide the avocado and mango slices among the plates. Scatter over the stir-fried prawns, drizzling over any extra dressing left in the wok to serve.

Crab, Avocado and Mango Salad

This is great for a leisurely lunch on a bright spring day or as a starter for a dinner party. All the components can be prepared an hour before serving, so it's perfect if you don't want to have too much to do at the last minute before your guests arrive.

50ml (2fl oz) low-fat mayonnaise

1 large, ripe avocado

2 tbsp tomato relish (preferably Ballymaloe)

1 tsp chopped fresh coriander

1 tbsp freshly squeezed lemon juice

1 tsp finely grated lemon rind

2 tbsp rapeseed oil

1 tsp clear honey

1 tsp balsamic vinegar

9 cherry tomatoes, quartered (preferably vine-ripened)

225g (8oz) fresh white crabmeat, well picked over

2 Little Gem lettuces, trimmed and shredded

1 small, firm, ripe mango, peeled and cut into thin strips

sea salt and freshly ground black pepper

fresh micro coriander, to garnish

SERVES 6

Set aside 4 teaspoons of the mayonnaise in a bowl to use as a garnish. Place 2 tablespoons of the remaining mayonnaise in a liquidizer or mini food processor. Cut the avocado in half and scoop out the flesh, then add to the food processor with 1 tablespoon of the tomato relish and the chopped coriander and blitz until smooth. Transfer to a bowl, cover with cling film and chill until needed.

Mix the reserved mayonnaise to use as a garnish with the remaining tablespoon of the tomato relish, the lemon juice and lemon rind. Place in a bowl, cover with cling film and chill until needed.

Mix together the rapeseed oil, honey and balsamic vinegar in a bowl and season to taste. Fold in the cherry tomatoes, cover with cling film and set aside at room temperature to allow the flavours to develop.

Using two forks, shred the crabmeat, discarding any pieces of shell.

To serve, spoon some of the avocado mayonnaise into the bottom of six glasses. Put a layer of the lettuce leaves on top, then scatter over the mango, followed by the marinated tomatoes. Spoon over the crabmeat in an even layer and garnish with the tomato mayonnaise and micro coriander. Set on plates to serve.

Three Tomato and Beetroot Salad with Harissa and Goat's Cheese

Boilíe goat's cheese is wonderfully creamy, yet has a mild flavour. It's made in Cavan just a couple of miles up the road from the restaurant. I love using it and find myself returning to it again and again.

400g (14oz) cooked baby beetroot, halved (drained from a jar or use the recipe for roasted beetroot on page 64)

100g (4oz) red cherry tomatoes, halved

100g (4oz) yellow cherry tomatoes, halved

100g (4oz) vine-ripened tomatoes, sliced into thin wedges

12 Boilíe goat's cheese balls, drained (from a jar)

1 tbsp toasted flaked almonds

DRESSING:

3 tbsp extra virgin olive oil

1 tbsp chopped fresh basil, plus extra sprigs to garnish

5 tsp balsamic vinegar

1 tsp harissa paste

finely grated rind of ½ lemon

sea salt and freshly ground black pepper

SERVES 4

To make the dressing, place all the ingredients in a large bowl and season with salt and pepper, then whisk until emulsified. Add the beetroot and various tomatoes and gently fold together to combine.

Divide the salad between four plates or put on one large platter and arrange the goat's cheese balls on top. Scatter over the toasted almonds and garnish with the basil sprigs to serve.

FISH

Fresh Tuna Niçoise

This classic salad is perfect for serving at a relaxed late lunch or supper party. The tuna is best cooked until medium-rare so that it remains moist, but cook it for a minute or two longer if you prefer. Or you could always use some good-quality canned tuna, preferably the kind that is preserved in olive oil.

TAPENADE:

100g (4oz) pitted black olives

15g (½oz) tinned anchovies, drained

1 small garlic clove, crushed

2 tbsp shredded fresh basil

1 tbsp rinsed capers

2 tsp olive oil

½ tsp lemon juice

DRESSING:

3 tbsp extra virgin olive oil

1 tsp Dijon mustard

1 tsp white wine vinegar

squeeze of lemon juice

SALAD:

300g (11oz) baby new potatoes

4 eggs

100g (4oz) green beans, trimmed

2 heads of Little Gem lettuce, trimmed and leaves roughly torn

24 baby plum cherry tomatoes, cut in half

16 pitted black olives

4 tsp rinsed capers

TUNA:

4 x 100g (4oz) fresh tuna steaks, each about 2.5cm (1in) thick

1 tbsp olive oil

sea salt and freshly ground black pepper

sourdough toasts, to serve

SERVES 4–6

To make the tapenade, place all the ingredients in a mini food processor and season with salt and pepper, then pulse until roughly chopped. Place in a dish, cover and set aside until needed.

To make the dressing, place all the ingredients in a screw-topped jar and season with salt and pepper. Put the lid on and shake really well until it's nice and thick.

Bring a medium pan of salted water to the boil. Add the potatoes, then cover, reduce the heat and simmer for 10–15 minutes, until just tender. Drain and leave them to cool completely, then cut them all in half.

Meanwhile, put the eggs in a small pan and just cover with boiling water. Place on a medium heat and bring to a simmer, then cook for 6 minutes. Drain and rinse under cold running water, then peel off the shells and cut each egg into quarters lengthways.

Plunge the green beans into a pan of boiling salted water and cook over a medium heat for 2–3 minutes to blanch. Drain and refresh under cold running water.

Heat a griddle pan or heavy-based frying pan over a very high heat for 5 minutes. Brush the tuna with the olive oil and season with salt and pepper. Cook for 2 minutes on each side, depending on how rare you want it. Leave to rest for a couple of minutes and then cut into slices.

Put the cooked baby new potatoes in a large bowl with the green beans, lettuce, cherry tomatoes, olives and capers. Add 2 tablespoons of the dressing and toss gently to coat. Arrange on plates or use one large platter. Arrange the slices of tuna on top and drizzle over the rest of the dressing. Finish with the quarters of soft-boiled eggs and serve with the tapenade and sourdough toasts.

Miso Grilled Hake with Avocado and Lime Salsa

The true flavour for this dish comes from the white miso paste, which is available in good delis and Asian stores. Also known as sweet or mellow miso, white miso is fermented for a shorter time and is lower in salt than the darker varieties. It has a milder, more delicate flavour, making it the perfect partner for fish.

4 x 200g (7oz) hake fillets, skinned and boned

rapeseed oil, for greasing

200g (7oz) mixed baby salad leaves

lime wedges, to garnish

MARINADE:

2 garlic cloves, crushed

4 tbsp white miso paste

1 tbsp freshly grated root ginger

1 tbsp maple syrup

1 tbsp rice wine vinegar

1 tbsp toasted sesame oil

SALSA:

100g (4oz) cherry tomatoes, cut into quarters

1 small red chilli, seeded and finely diced

finely grated zest and juice of 1 lime

1 tbsp olive oil

1 tbsp chopped fresh coriander

1 small, firm, ripe avocado, peeled, stoned and diced

sea salt and freshly ground black pepper

SERVES 4

Mix all the marinade ingredients together in a non-metallic shallow dish. Place the hake in the marinade, turning to coat. Cover with cling film and place in the fridge for a couple of hours or overnight is fine.

Preheat the oven to 180°C (350°F/gas mark 4). Line a baking sheet with parchment paper and brush the paper with a little rapeseed oil.

Arrange the marinated hake on top of the oiled paper, skinned side down. Spoon over 2 tablespoons of the marinade and bake for 12–15 minutes, until the hake is just cooked through and tender. The exact cooking time will depend on the thickness of the fillets.

Meanwhile, to make the salsa, place the cherry tomatoes, red chilli, lime zest and juice, olive oil and coriander in a bowl. Mix together and season with salt and pepper, then carefully stir in the avocado. Do not over mix.

Preheat the grill to medium. Remove the hake from the oven and brush over the rest of the marinade, then place under the grill for 2–3 minutes, until golden, being careful that the parchment paper does not catch and begin to burn.

Arrange the salad leaves on plates with the avocado and cherry tomato salsa. Top each plate with a piece of hake and add a lime wedge to each one to serve.

Spicy Prawn Cakes with Ginger

This is my twist on some classic South-East Asian street food that I enjoyed on a recent trip to the region. As many people there are gluten intolerant, they would dust the cakes in cornflour instead of regular flour before frying. It's also important to leave some texture in the raw mixture or the end result can become a bit tough and rubbery.

PRAWN CAKES:

300g (11oz) raw peeled tiger prawns, deveined

100g (4oz) whiting, skinned and boned

1 egg

1 garlic clove, crushed

1 red chilli, seeded and finely chopped

3 tbsp chopped fresh coriander

1 tbsp sweet chilli sauce

1 tsp freshly grated root ginger

1 tsp toasted sesame oil

plain flour, for dusting

2 tbsp rapeseed oil

DRESSING:

2 tbsp rapeseed oil

1 tbsp freshly grated root ginger

1 small leek, trimmed and thinly sliced (about 200g (7oz))

1 tbsp water

2 tbsp light soy sauce

1 tbsp white wine vinegar

1 tbsp toasted sesame oil

1 tbsp toasted sesame seeds

1 tsp palm sugar

TO SERVE:

rice noodles or fragrant rice

lime wedges

1 spring onion, thinly sliced, to garnish

fresh coriander leaves, to garnish

SERVES 4

Dry the prawns and whiting in kitchen paper and then roughly chop. Place in a food processor with the egg and pulse until it has a rough texture. Add the remaining prawn cake ingredients except for the flour and rapeseed oil and pulse for 10 seconds, until just combined – you want to keep some texture.

Tip the mixture onto a floured surface and with floured hands shape into 8 rounds, each about 1cm (1/2in) thick. You can make these ahead and put them on a plate covered with cling film in the fridge for up to 24 hours.

Heat the rapeseed oil in a large non-stick frying pan over a medium heat. Fry the prawn cakes for 3–4 minutes on each side, until golden, turning once.

Meanwhile, to make the dressing, heat a separate non-stick frying pan over a medium heat. Add 1 tablespoon of the rapeseed oil, then add the ginger and sauté for 30 seconds. Add the leek and sprinkle over the water. Cook for 5 minutes, tossing occasionally. Mix the rest of the ingredients together in a small bowl, including the remaining tablespoon of oil, and season with salt and pepper, then remove the leek from the heat and stir it into the dressing.

To serve, spoon some fragrant rice onto each plate and arrange two of the spicy prawn cakes on top. Put the dressing into small bowls and serve alongside with a lime wedge. Garnish with spring onions and coriander.

Sea Bass with Ginger and Chilli

The ginger and chilli dressing is perfect for fish, but it would also taste great with some simply grilled chicken or pork or steamed pak choy, which is now grown very successfully in Ireland, believe it or not!

4 x 150g (5oz) sea bass fillets, skin on and bones removed (scaled)

2 tbsp rapeseed oil

2.5cm (1in) piece of fresh root ginger, peeled and cut into thin strips

2 garlic cloves, thinly sliced

1 red chilli, seeded and thinly sliced

2 spring onions, finely shredded lengthways

1 tbsp soy sauce

sea salt and freshly ground black pepper

steamed fragrant rice, to serve

fresh micro coriander leaves, to garnish

SERVES 4

Season the sea bass fillets with salt and pepper, then slash the skin of each one three times.

Heat a large non-stick frying pan over a medium heat and add 1 tablespoon of the rapeseed oil. Add the sea bass fillets to the pan, skin side down, and cook for 5 minutes, until the skin is crispy and golden, pressing down gently with a fish slice if the fillets begin to curl at the edges. The fish will almost be cooked at this point, so just turn it over and cook for 1 minute more. Transfer to a plate and keep warm. You will have to cook the fish in two batches to cook it correctly.

Wipe out the frying pan, then return it to the heat and add the remaining tablespoon of oil. Add the ginger, garlic and chilli and stir-fry for 2 minutes, until golden. Remove from the heat and add the spring onions and soy sauce, swirling to combine.

To serve, place the sea bass fillets on plates and spoon over the ginger and chilli dressing from the pan. Add a small mound of rice to each plate and scatter over the micro coriander.

Grilled Sardines with Salsa Verde

These simply grilled sardines are delightfully delicious, but only buy them when they are extremely fresh – stiff fresh, as they say in the fishmonger trade. In my opinion, frozen sardines are such a disappointment. You're left thinking how horrible oily fish are, when in fact that isn't true. If unavailable, fresh small mackerel, herrings or even sprats are a good substitute.

8–20 fresh sardines
(depending on their size)

1 tbsp extra virgin olive oil,
plus extra for greasing

cherry tomato and red onion salad,
to serve

lightly dressed green salad, to serve

SALSA VERDE:

4 pitted green olives, finely chopped

1 garlic clove, finely chopped

2 tbsp extra virgin olive oil

1 tbsp chopped fresh flat-leaf parsley

2 tsp rinsed baby capers (or use
regular-sized capers and cut them in half)

1 tsp finely grated lemon zest

1 tsp chopped fresh rosemary

sea salt and freshly ground black pepper

SERVES 4

You only need to gut the sardines if they weigh more than 65g (2 1/2oz) or if they are longer than 13cm (5in). Otherwise you can leave them as they are. Rub the scales off under cold running water and dry on kitchen paper.

Preheat the grill to high. Arrange the sardines on a lightly oiled sturdy baking sheet. Drizzle over the extra virgin olive oil and season with salt and pepper. Grill for 2–4 minutes on each side, until cooked through and tender. The exact cooking time will depend on their size.

Meanwhile, to make the salsa verde, mix together all the ingredients and season with salt.

Remove the sardines from the grill and spoon the salsa verde down the middle of them. Put the baking sheet straight on the table with a plate of tomato and red onion salad and a separate bowl of green salad.

CHICKEN

Garlic and Lemon Chicken with Rocket

This is the kind of dinner I make again and again at home. The combination of flavours is just sublime and it really takes no time at all to prepare.

3 tbsp lemon rapeseed oil

4 shallots, peeled and halved

2 large garlic bulbs, halved

4 boneless chicken breasts, skin on

1 lemon, cut in half lengthways and sliced

4 fresh thyme sprigs

sea salt and freshly ground black pepper

lightly dressed rocket and green bean salad, to serve

SERVES 4

Preheat the oven to 180°C (350°F/gas mark 4).

Heat 1 tablespoon of the lemon rapeseed oil in a non-stick frying pan over a low heat. Add the shallots and garlic and sauté for 5 minutes, until they begin to catch some colour. Transfer to a small roasting tin.

Increase the heat under the frying pan to high, add another tablespoon of the oil and quickly seal the chicken breasts for 2 minutes on each side, until browned. Transfer the chicken breasts to the small roasting tin, tucking them around the shallots and garlic, then tuck in the lemon slices and thyme sprigs. Season with salt and pepper, then drizzle over the remaining tablespoon of the lemon rapeseed oil. Place in the oven for 15–20 minutes, until the chicken breasts are cooked through.

Remove the chicken from the oven and cover loosely with foil for 5 minutes to allow the chicken to rest, then serve straight to the table with the rocket and green bean salad.

Chicken Kiev with Sweet Potato Chips

Reduce the calorie count – and the guilt factor –
of the classic Kiev with this baked version.

50g (2oz) butter, softened

2 garlic cloves, crushed

finely grated rind and juice of ½ lemon

1 tbsp snipped fresh chives

1 tbsp chopped fresh flat-leaf parsley

½ tsp cayenne pepper

4 skinless chicken breast fillets

50g (2oz) plain flour

2 eggs

150g (5oz) fresh granary breadcrumbs

about 1 tsp olive oil spray

lightly dressed spinach salad, to serve

SWEET POTATO CHIPS:

2 large sweet potatoes, peeled and cut into thick chips

1 tbsp olive oil

¼ tsp crushed dried chillies

sea salt and freshly ground black pepper

SERVES 4

Mix together the butter, garlic, lemon rind and juice, chives, parsley and cayenne pepper. Season with salt and pepper and mix well to combine.

Using a sharp knife, carefully cut a small hole at the fattest end of each chicken breast. Push the knife into the middle of the chicken breast, making sure not to cut through the chicken. Keep working the knife around to make an opening just large enough to get the butter into. Using a small spoon or piping bag, fill each of the chicken breasts with one-quarter of the butter. Don't try to overfill the chicken cavity or the butter might seep out while it is cooking.

Place the flour on a plate and season with salt and pepper. Beat the eggs in a shallow dish and place the breadcrumbs in a separate shallow dish. Dust the chicken breasts in the seasoned flour, then dip them into the beaten eggs, shaking off any excess. Finally, roll them into the granary breadcrumbs until they are evenly coated all over. Arrange the coated chicken breasts on a tray lined with parchment paper and spray lightly with the olive oil. Place in the fridge for at least 1 hour to allow the butter to harden up.

Preheat the oven to 190°C (375°F/gas mark 5).

Toss the sweet potatoes in the olive oil on a baking sheet, then sprinkle with the chilli flakes and salt. Arrange in a single layer and roast on the top shelf of the oven for 20–25 minutes, until cooked through and golden.

Put the prepared chicken into the oven and roast for
20–25 minutes, until cooked through.

Remove the chicken Kievs from the oven and leave to
settle and rest for 5 minutes. Arrange on plates with the
sweet potato chips and serve with a separate bowl of
spinach salad.

Chicken Tabbouleh Salad with Tahini Drizzle

This tasty chicken salad is made with cracked wheat, also known as bulgar or burghul wheat. You'll find it in health food shops or alongside the dried pulses and beans in the supermarket.

250g (9oz) bulgur wheat

500ml (18fl oz) boiling water

1 tbsp lemon rapeseed oil

3 small skinless chicken breast fillets

20 cherry tomatoes, cut in half (preferably vine-ripened)

4 spring onions, trimmed and thinly sliced

2 roasted red peppers, cut into thin strips (from a jar or a can)

1 small red onion, thinly sliced

1 x 400g (14oz) can of chickpeas, drained and rinsed

2 tbsp roughly chopped fresh flat-leaf parsley

1 tbsp roughly chopped fresh mint

finely grated rind and juice of 1 lemon

2 tbsp extra virgin olive oil

TAHINI DRIZZLE:

3 tbsp thick Greek yoghurt

1 tbsp light tahini (sesame seed paste)

5 tbsp water

sea salt and freshly ground black pepper

SERVES 4

Place the bulgur wheat in a bowl and pour over the boiling water. Cover with cling film and set aside for 20 minutes, until the wheat is soft and all the liquid has been absorbed.

Meanwhile, place the lemon rapeseed oil in a large non-stick frying pan over a medium heat. Season the chicken breasts with salt and pepper and cook for 10-12 minutes, until cooked through and tender, turning once. Remove from the heat and leave to rest for 5 minutes before cutting into slices.

Place the tomatoes, spring onions, red peppers, red onion, chickpeas and herbs in a large bowl, then fold in the bulgur wheat and dress with the lemon rind and juice and the extra virgin olive oil. Arrange the slices of chicken on top.

To make the tahini drizzle, mix the yoghurt and tahini in a small bowl and season generously. Pour in enough water to make a dressing consistency and then drizzle over the salad. Serve straight to the table and allow everyone to help themselves.

Cashew Nut Chicken and Asparagus Salad with Mango Salsa

This delicious salad is packed full of goodness. It can be served simple and rustic, or for a more formal occasion you can spoon the mango salsa into 10cm (4in) chef's rings set on plates. Arrange the crispy cashew nut chicken in the middle and garnish with a small mound of dressed baby salad leaves. Remove the chef's rings to serve.

100g (4oz) panko
(dried toasted breadcrumbs)

75g (3oz) toasted cashew nuts

25g (1oz) toasted coconut flakes

50g (2oz) plain flour

1 egg

50ml (2fl oz) milk

2 x 200g (7oz) chicken fillets,
sliced lengthways

about 1 tsp olive oil spray

1 bunch of asparagus

2 baby Cos lettuces

1 small head of radicchio lettuce

alfalfa sprouts, to garnish

MANGO SALSA:

1 firm, ripe mango, peeled and diced

1 small red onion, finely diced

juice of ½ lime

1 tbsp rapeseed oil

1 tbsp chopped fresh coriander

sea salt and freshly ground black pepper

SERVES 4

Preheat the oven to 180°C (350°F/gas mark 4). Line a baking sheet with parchment paper.

Place the panko, cashew nuts and coconut flakes in a food processor with a pinch of salt. Blend for 2–3 minutes, then tip into a shallow dish.

Place the flour in a dish and season with salt and pepper. Whisk the egg and milk together in a separate dish. Dust each slice of chicken in the seasoned flour, then dip into the egg wash and coat in the cashew nut crumbs.

Place the coated chicken strips on the lined baking sheet and spray lightly with the olive oil. Place in the oven for 15–20 minutes, until cooked through and golden.

Meanwhile, to make the mango salsa, mix the mango with the red onion, lime juice, rapeseed oil and coriander, then season to taste and set aside at room temperature.

Break the woody stems off the asparagus and cut each one on the diagonal into two or three pieces, depending on their size. Blanch in a pan of boiling salted water for 2–3 minutes, until just tender but still with a little bite. Drain and refresh under cold running water.

Trim down the Cos lettuces and radicchio, then break into separate leaves and put in a large bowl with the blanched asparagus. Arrange in shallow bowls and place the cashew nut chicken strips on top. Spoon around the mango salsa and add the alfalfa sprouts to garnish.

Baked Chicken and Chorizo Rice with Artichokes

This one-pot wonder gives maximum flavour with minimum effort and is guaranteed to wake up your taste buds. I like to serve it with sautéed spinach to make sure I'm getting plenty of greens. If you don't have a suitable casserole dish, just use a large sauté pan, then transfer to a roasting tin and cover loosely with foil. Make sure you buy the raw chorizo for this dish, which will impart lots of flavour into the rice as it cooks.

1 x 300g (11oz) jar of artichoke hearts preserved in olive oil

4 chicken breast fillets, skin on

100g (4oz) raw chorizo sausage, peeled and diced

1 large onion, finely chopped

2 garlic cloves, crushed

350g (12oz) long-grain rice

150ml (¼ pint) dry white wine

600ml (1 pint) chicken stock

200g (7oz) baby spinach leaves

2 tbsp roughly chopped fresh flat-leaf parsley

sea salt and freshly ground black pepper

SERVES 4

Preheat the oven to 180°C (350°F/gas mark 4).

Drain the oil from the jar of artichokes. Add 1 tablespoon of this oil to a casserole dish with a lid, then place on the hob over a medium to high heat. Season the chicken breasts and add them to the dish, skin side down. Cook for 2–3 minutes, until lightly browned. Turn over and cook for another minute or so, until sealed. Transfer to a plate and set aside.

Add another tablespoon of the drained artichoke oil to the dish, then tip in the chorizo, onion and garlic. Sauté for 2–3 minutes, until the onion has softened but not coloured. Add the rice and cook for another 2 minutes, stirring, until the chorizo has begun to release its oil and all the rice grains are well coated.

Pour the wine into the casserole dish, stirring to combine, then add the stock and fold in the artichokes. Arrange the chicken on top, pushing the breasts down into the rice. Cover and bake for 30–35 minutes, until all the liquid has been absorbed and the chicken and rice are cooked through and tender.

Remove the chicken breasts and stir in the spinach until it has just wilted. Return the chicken breasts to the dish, then scatter over the parsley and place directly on the table to serve.

PORK

Orange and Thyme Pork Steaks with Winter Slaw

The combination of the sweet, almost caramelised pork with the tangy butter-milk dressing for the winter slaw is absolutely delicious. It's a recipe you'll find yourself making again and again and the whole thing can be prepared from start to finish in well under half an hour. It's best to use a mandolin for the winter slaw, but a food processor with a blade attachment will also do the trick.

1 tbsp olive oil

1 tbsp finely shredded orange rind

1 tsp fresh thyme leaves

4 x 175g (6oz) pork loin steaks

4 tbsp freshly squeezed orange juice

1 tbsp maple syrup

WINTER SLAW:

1 small celeriac, peeled and cut into julienne (on a mandolin)

1 fennel bulb, thinly sliced

¼ head of crisp green cabbage, core removed and thinly sliced

good handful of fresh flat-leaf parsley leaves

4 tbsp buttermilk

1 tbsp fresh lemon juice

sea salt and freshly ground black pepper

SERVES 4

To make the winter slaw, place the celeriac, fennel, cabbage and parsley in a bowl and toss to combine. Stir in the buttermilk and lemon juice and season to taste. Set aside until needed.

Heat a frying pan over a high heat. Add the oil, then tip in the orange rind and thyme. Cook for 1–2 minutes, until crisp but not burnt – be careful, as the orange rind and thyme may spit a little when added to the pan. Remove from the pan with a slotted spoon and set aside.

Season the pork steaks and add them to the same frying pan. Reduce the heat to medium and cook for 3–4 minutes on each side, until cooked through and nicely golden. Remove from the pan and set aside.

Pour the orange juice into the pan and drizzle over the maple syrup. Simmer for 1 minute, until slightly reduced. Return the pork steaks and the orange rind mixture to the pan and cook the pork for another minute on each side, until heated through.

Arrange the pork steaks on warmed serving plates and spoon over the juices from the pan. Add a portion of winter slaw to each one to serve.

Pork Goulash with Cauliflower Rice

Goulash was one of my mom's regular dinners when I was growing up, and I loved it. I now like to serve it with cauliflower rice, which has a similar texture to rice but a much lower GI. Contrary to popular belief, a true goulash doesn't contain any soured cream, making for a much healthier dinner.

2 tbsp plain flour

2 tsp smoked paprika

500g (1lb 2oz) pork stir-fry strips

2 tbsp olive oil

2 onions, thinly sliced

2 green peppers, cored and cut into slices

1 garlic clove, finely chopped

1 tsp dried oregano

120ml (4 floz) red wine

1 x 400g (14oz) can of chopped tomatoes

200ml (7fl oz) beef or chicken stock

2 tbsp Worcestershire sauce

1 tbsp tomato purée

1 tsp honey

2 tbsp chopped fresh flat-leaf parsley

CAULIFLOWER RICE:

1 head of cauliflower

sea salt and freshly ground black pepper

SERVES 4–6

Place the flour and smoked paprika in a bowl and season with salt and pepper. Use this to evenly coat the pork strips, tipping away any excess flour.

Heat 1 tablespoon of the olive oil in a flameproof casserole over a medium heat and quickly brown the pork on all sides. Don't put too much pork in the casserole at once or it won't brown – it's best to fry it in batches. Transfer the meat to a plate and set aside.

Add the remaining tablespoon of oil to the casserole, then sauté the onions, green peppers, garlic and dried oregano for about 5 minutes, until the vegetables are just beginning to catch a bit of colour. Return the pork to the casserole and stir to combine. Pour in the wine and allow it to bubble down, scraping the bottom of the casserole with a wooden spoon to remove any sediment. Add the tomatoes, stock, Worcestershire sauce, tomato purée, honey and a good pinch of sea salt and black pepper and bring up to a steady simmer. Place the lid on the casserole and simmer for another 20 minutes or so, until the pork is completely tender.

Meanwhile, to make the cauliflower rice, cut the hard core and stalks from the cauliflower and pulse the rest in a food processor to make grains the size of rice. Line the base of a steamer with parchment paper, tip in the cauliflower and cook for 8–10 minutes, until tender. Season with salt and pepper, then fluff up with a fork.

Divide the cauliflower rice among warmed plates, then spoon over the pork goulash. Garnish with the parsley to serve.

Parma-Wrapped Pork Fillet with Pesto and Stir-Fried Curly Kale

The crispy, salty flavour of the Parma ham blends well with the natural sweetness of the pesto and makes the pork all the more succulent. This recipe is also delicious made with Serrano ham. Be generous when stuffing the pork – a bit of the pesto smeared on the outside is fine if you've got any left over.

2 x 400g (14oz) pieces of pork fillet, trimmed

12 thin slices of Parma ham (about 225g (8oz) in total)

PESTO:

50g (2oz) pine nuts

bunch of fresh basil, leaves stripped

2 fresh sage leaves

1 garlic clove, peeled

100g (4oz) Pecorino cheese, finely grated

about 7 tbsp extra virgin olive oil

KALE:

1 tbsp olive oil

200g (7oz) curly kale

2 tbsp water

1 mild red chilli, seeded and thinly sliced

2 garlic cloves, thinly sliced

sea salt and freshly ground black pepper

SERVES 4–6

Preheat the oven to 200°C (400°F/gas mark 6).

To make the pesto, heat a small heavy-based frying pan over a medium heat. Add the pine nuts and cook until golden brown, tossing occasionally. Tip out onto a plate and leave to cool completely. When cool, place in a food processor with the basil, sage, garlic and Pecorino. Blend briefly and then pour in enough olive oil through the feeder tube to make a thick purée. Blend once more, then season with salt and pepper.

Place one of the pork fillets on a chopping board with the thickest part facing you and ram the handle of a large wooden spoon through its length. Put the pesto in a piping bag fitted with a 2cm ($3/4$ in) plain nozzle and pipe the pesto into the hole made in the fillet. Alternatively, you could insert the pesto with a teaspoon. Wrap the fillet in half of the Parma ham – if it doesn't stay wrapped together properly, tie it with kitchen string at 2.5cm (1in) intervals. Repeat with the second pork fillet.

Place both Parma-wrapped pork fillets in a roasting tin and cover with foil. Bake for 15 minutes, then remove the foil and cook for another 5 minutes, until the pork is cooked through, the juices run clear when a skewer is inserted and the Parma ham is crispy. Remove from the oven and leave to rest for 5 minutes in a warm place.

Meanwhile, to prepare the kale, heat the oil in a large wok, then add the kale and sprinkle over the water. Season, then stir-fry for 4 minutes. Add the chilli and garlic and continue to stir-fry for another 2 minutes, until the kale is tender and vibrant green. Remove from the heat.

Carve the rested pork into slices and arrange on plates with the kale to serve.

Spanish Meatball and Butter Bean Stew

These meatballs seem to taste even better when made a day ahead. Haricot or cannellini beans would also work well for this dish, as would minced turkey, or you could use a mixture. Butter beans are a large, creamy-coloured pulse that have a soft, floury texture and make for a very satisfying meal.

2 tbsp olive oil

2 red peppers, cored and sliced

1 red onion, sliced

1 tbsp water

2 large garlic cloves, finely chopped

1 tbsp sweet smoked paprika

2 x 400g (14oz) cans of chopped tomatoes

1 heaped tbsp tomato purée

1 x 400g (14oz) can of butter beans, drained and rinsed

MEATBALLS:

450g (1lb) lean minced pork

1 small onion, grated

4 tbsp fresh wholemeal breadcrumbs

1 tbsp tomato purée

1 heaped tbsp chopped fresh flat-leaf parsley, plus extra to garnish

sourdough bread, to serve (optional)

sea salt and freshly ground black pepper

SERVES 4

Heat the olive oil in a sauté pan over a medium-high heat. Add the peppers and red onion and sauté for about 5 minutes, until they are just beginning to soften. Sprinkle over a tablespoon of water to help them along. Stir in the garlic and paprika and cook for 1 minute. Add the tomatoes and tomato purée, then season with salt and pepper. Cover with a lid and simmer for 10 minutes.

Meanwhile, make the meatballs. Place the minced pork in a bowl with the grated onion, breadcrumbs, tomato purée, parsley and salt and pepper to taste. Mix until evenly combined, then shape into small, even-sized meatballs. Carefully add to the simmering tomato sauce along with the butter beans. Cover again, then reduce the heat and simmer gently for another 15 minutes, until the meatballs are cooked through and tender.

Ladle into bowls and scatter over a little extra parsley to garnish. Serve with some sourdough bread, if liked.

Chinese Pork and Three Pepper Stir-Fry

Stir-fries are a great way to prepare vegetables, as you only need to use a very small amount of oil and then steam-fry with a couple tablespoons of water. This cooks the vegetables nice and quickly without allowing them to stew.

2 tbsp sesame oil

400g (14oz) pork stir-fry strips

2.5cm (1in) piece of fresh root ginger, peeled and thinly sliced

2 garlic cloves, thinly sliced

1 mild red chilli, seeded and thinly sliced

1 red pepper, cored, seeded and sliced

1 yellow pepper, cored, seeded and sliced

1 green pepper, cored, seeded and sliced

200g (7oz) fine green beans, trimmed

1–2 tbsp water

75g (3oz) toasted cashew nuts

steamed brown rice, to serve

2 tbsp chopped fresh coriander

SAUCE:

2 tbsp dark soy sauce

2 tbsp oyster sauce

1 tbsp honey

1 tbsp toasted sesame seeds

juice of 1 lime

SERVES 4

Heat 1 tablespoon of the sesame oil in a non-stick wok or pan over a high heat. Add the pork stir-fry strips and cook in batches until they are sealed and evenly browned. Transfer to a colander with a slotted spoon while you cook the remainder. This will help drain off any excess oil.

Add the remaining tablespoon of oil to the wok and reduce the heat to medium, then stir-fry the ginger, garlic and chilli for 2 minutes. Tip in the peppers and green beans and stir-fry for another 5 minutes, sprinkling over a little water as necessary.

Quickly mix together all the sauce ingredients in a small bowl. Add the stir-fried pork strips back into the wok, then drizzle over the sauce, tossing to coat. Stir-fry for another minute or two, until everything is heated through. Add the cashew nuts and toss again to evenly coat.

Place some rice in each deep serving bowl and divide the pork stir-fry on top. Scatter over the coriander to serve.

BEEF

Beef Kofta Curry

These delicious koftas show how versatile minced beef can be and are bursting with ginger, cumin and fresh coriander. You can also make this curry using turkey mince with equally successful results.

1 tbsp rapeseed oil

1 green chilli, seeded and finely chopped

1 tbsp garam masala

2 tsp freshly grated root ginger

1 tsp ground turmeric

1 x 500ml (18fl oz) carton of passata
(Italian sieved tomatoes)

sea salt and freshly ground black pepper

toasted flaked almonds, to garnish

KOFTAS:

500g (1lb 2oz) lean minced beef

1 small onion, grated

2 tbsp chopped fresh coriander,
plus extra to garnish

2 tsp freshly grated root ginger

1 tsp cumin seeds

SOCCA FLATBREADS:

350g (12oz) chickpea flour

1 tsp fine sea salt

4 tbsp extra virgin olive oil

about 400ml (14fl oz) soda water

olive oil, for cooking

SERVES 4–6

To make the koftas, place the minced beef in a bowl with the grated onion, coriander, ginger and cumin seeds and season with a pinch of salt and a good grinding of black pepper. Mix until evenly combined, then with dampened hands, divide into 20 even-sized balls.

Heat the rapeseed oil a large pan wide enough to take the koftas in an even layer with a lid. Add the green chilli, garam masala, ginger and turmeric, stirring to combine. Cook for 30 seconds to 1 minute, until fragrant, then pour in the passata. Bring to the boil, then reduce the heat and season to taste.

Add the koftas to the pan in a single even layer, then cover and cook gently for 25–30 minutes. Gently shake the pan occasionally to ensure the koftas aren't sticking to the base of the pan, but don't stir. Using a tongs, turn the koftas over, then shake the pan gently and continue to cook with the lid off for 5 minutes, until the sauce has thickened slightly.

Meanwhile, make the socca flatbreads. Place the chickpea flour and salt in a large bowl and make a well in the centre, then slowly whisk in the extra virgin olive oil and enough of the soda water until you have achieved a smooth batter. Put a thin film of regular olive oil in a large non-stick frying pan and place over a high heat. When it's really hot and almost smoking, ladle in one-quarter of the batter, swirling it around so that it is evenly distributed.

Cook the socca flatbread over the high heat for 1 minute, then reduce the heat to medium and cook for another 2–3 minutes, until the base is set and the top looks like

it is drying out. Carefully flip over and cook for another couple of minutes. When the flatbread is cooked, carefully slide it off the pan and cover loosely with foil while you make the remainder.

To serve, ladle the beef kofta curry into bowls and garnish with the coriander and almonds. Set the bowl on a plate and put a separate plate of the socca flatbreads in the middle so that everyone can help themselves.

Vietnamese Beef Noodle Soup (Pho Bo)

I first had this in Saigon, where it can literally be found on every street corner. It is normally eaten for lunch there, but I think it's a fantastic option for a light, fresh supper. Serve it as they do in Vietnam, with a plateful of herbs such as Asian basil and mint, beansprouts and green chillies, which diners can then add to taste.

1.25 litres (2 ¼ pints) light beef stock (homemade or use 2 stock cubes made up with the correct quantity of water)

2.5cm (1in) piece of fresh root ginger, peeled and sliced

2 whole star anise (optional)

1 cinnamon stick

225g (8oz) Thai flat rice noodles (try to use the Thai Gold brand)

225g (8oz) beef sirloin steak, trimmed of any fat and slightly frozen

3 tbsp Thai fish sauce (nam pla)

good pinch of freshly ground black pepper

100g (4oz) fresh beansprouts

4 spring onions, trimmed and finely chopped

2 red or green Thai bird's eye chillies, thinly sliced

1 small bunch of fresh coriander, leaves stripped and finely chopped

handful of fresh basil leaves, torn

handful of fresh mint leaves, torn

lime wedges, to garnish

SERVES 4–6

Pour the stock into a large pan and add the ginger, star anise, if using, and the cinnamon stick. Bring to the boil, then reduce the heat and simmer for 15 minutes.

Soak the noodles in a large bowl with enough boiling water to cover them for 15 minutes, or until they are softened and pliable. Drain the noodles in a colander, then place in a pan of boiling water and simmer for 45 seconds, until tender, or according to the packet instructions. Drain well and set aside.

Meanwhile, using a very sharp knife, cut the sirloin across the grain into very thin slices. Strain the flavoured stock into a clean pan and heat to a simmer. Stir in the Thai fish sauce and the black pepper. Add the sliced sirloin steak and simmer for 30–45 seconds, until the meat loses its redness. Skim off any froth from the soup.

Divide the noodles among four large, warmed bowls and place a pile of beansprouts on top of each one. Ladle over the flavoured beef broth and sprinkle the spring onions, chillies, coriander, basil and mint on top. Garnish with the lime wedges to serve.

Minute Steaks with White Bean Purée and Sautéed Savoy Cabbage

This white bean purée is a great alternative to creamy mashed potatoes and is every bit as moreish. I have served it here with some minute steaks, which literally take 3 minutes to cook. Savoy cabbage provides some excellent colour and texture to the dish, but you could always use another variety, such as York or January King, depending on what's available.

3 tbsp extra virgin olive oil

2 tsp finely chopped fresh rosemary

2 tsp finely chopped fresh thyme

4 x 150g (5oz) thin-cut sirloin steaks

1 onion, finely chopped

2 garlic cloves, crushed

2 x 400g (14oz) cans of cannellini beans, drained and rinsed

good pinch of caraway seeds

1 small Savoy cabbage, cored and shredded

about 6 tbsp chicken stock

1 tbsp chopped fresh flat-leaf parsley

1 tbsp snipped fresh chives

sea salt and freshly ground black pepper

SERVES 4

Place 1 tablespoon of the olive oil in a shallow non-metallic dish. Add the rosemary and most of the thyme, then season generously with black pepper. Add the minute steaks, turning to coat, then either use immediately or cover with cling film and chill for up to 24 hours – just make sure you allow them to come back to room temperature before cooking, if time allows.

Heat a heavy-based frying pan until smoking hot. Add the minute steaks and cook for 1 1/2 minutes on each side, until well sealed. Remove from the heat and leave to rest in a warm place for about 5 minutes.

Meanwhile, heat another tablespoon of olive oil in a heavy-based pan over a low heat. Add the onion and garlic and cook gently for 2–3 minutes, until softened but not coloured, stirring occasionally. Stir in the cannellini beans and cook for another few minutes, until they are heated through.

To sauté the cabbage, heat a wok or large frying pan and add the remaining tablespoon of olive oil. Sauté the caraway seeds for 20 seconds or so, then tip in the cabbage with the rest of the thyme and sauté for 1–2 minutes, until softened but not coloured. Pour in a couple tablespoons of the stock, season generously and allow to cook for another few minutes, until almost all of the liquid has evaporated, stirring.

Stir the rest of the stock into the bean mixture and mash to a rough purée using a potato masher or fork. Fold in the parsley and chives, then season to taste.

Divide the bean purée among four warmed serving plates and arrange the rested minute steaks on top, drizzling over any juices from the pan. Add a mound of cabbage to each one to serve.

Roast Rolled Rib of Beef with Horseradish Crème Fraîche

This is a great way to have a Sunday roast but without the guilt, particularly when served with roasted root vegetables. Ask your butcher for a cube roll of beef, which is an excellent cut for roasting and perfect when you've got to feed a crowd. Always allow a joint to come back up to room temperature before roasting to achieve the best flavour.

1.5kg (3 ¼lb) rolled cube of rib beef
2 tbsp olive oil
2 onions, roughly chopped
2 carrots, roughly chopped
2 celery sticks, roughly chopped
2 tsp potato flour
300ml (½ pint) beef stock
roasted root vegetables, to serve

HORSERADISH CRÈME FRAÎCHE:
5 tbsp crème fraîche
1 tbsp creamed horseradish
1 tsp Dijon mustard
1 tsp snipped fresh chives
sea salt and freshly ground black pepper

SERVES 8–10

Preheat the oven to 220°C (425°F/gas mark 7).

Wipe the meat with damp kitchen paper and drizzle with 1 tablespoon of the olive oil. Season well with salt and pepper, rubbing it all over the meat. Pour the remaining tablespoon of olive oil into a roasting tin and heat in the oven for 5 minutes. Add the onions, carrots and celery, tossing to coat. Season to taste and roast for 15 minutes.

Reduce the oven temperature to 190°C (375°F/gas mark 5). Remove the roasting tin from the oven and sit the beef on the bed of vegetables. Roast the beef for 1 hour for medium. If you prefer it medium rare, take it out 5–10 minutes earlier. For well done, leave it in for another 10–15 minutes.

Meanwhile, to make the horseradish crème fraîche, mix all the ingredients in a serving bowl and season with salt and pepper, then cover with cling film and chill until needed.

Remove the beef from the tin and place on a large dish. Rest in a warm place for at least 20 minutes before carving. To make the gravy, stir the potato flour into the juices in the roasting tin and then gradually stir in the stock. Place directly on the hob to simmer for 5 minutes, stirring and scraping the bottom with a wooden spoon to release any sediment. Season and pour through a sieve

into a gravy boat, discarding the vegetables that the beef
has been roasted on.

Carve the beef into slices and arrange on warmed plates.
Serve with roasted root vegetables and hand round the
gravy and horseradish crème fraîche separately.

Chargrilled Thai Beef Salad

The people of Thailand and neighbouring countries are very fond of this salad. This is an authentic recipe I picked up on my travels and have enjoyed cooking back here at home. It's also very good with prawns.

1 tsp jasmine rice

2 dried small red chillies

500g (1lb 2oz) thick beef fillet

3 tbsp ketjap manis (sweet soy sauce)

1 tbsp toasted sesame oil

100g (4oz) cherry tomatoes, halved

4 red shallots, thinly sliced

4 spring onions, trimmed and thinly sliced

1 small cucumber, peeled, halved, seeded and cut into 1cm (½in) slices

1 mild red chilli, seeded and thinly sliced

handful of fresh mint leaves

handful of fresh coriander leaves

small handful of fresh basil leaves, torn

2 tsp palm sugar

4 tbsp fresh lime juice

3 tbsp Thai fish sauce (nam pla)

100g (4oz) mixed green salad leaves

SERVES 4–6

If using a charcoal barbecue to grill the beef, light it 30 minutes before you want to start cooking. If using a gas barbecue, light it 10 minutes beforehand. Alternatively, use a griddle or frying pan.

Heat a dry frying pan, add the rice and toast until golden but not burnt. Grind the rice in a coffee grinder or pound to a powder in a pestle and mortar and set aside.

Reheat the frying pan and add the dried chillies. Toast until they are smoky, tossing regularly, then grind or pound to a powder. Mix in a small bowl with the rice and set aside – you should have about 2 teaspoons in total.

If using a griddle or frying pan, place it over a high heat until it's very hot. Cook the beef fillet over medium-hot coals on the barbecue or on the pan for 10–12 minutes, until well marked on the outside and rare to medium-rare inside. Place in a non-metallic bowl and leave to rest for 10 minutes, then mix together the ketjap manis and sesame oil and brush it all over the fillet. Cover with cling film and leave to marinate in a cool place for 2 hours, turning from time to time. This is not essential but it really does help the flavours to develop and the beef to properly rest.

Place the cherry tomatoes, shallots, spring onions, cucumber, chilli and herbs in a large bowl and gently toss together to combine. Cover with cling film and chill until needed.

Dissolve the palm sugar in a screw-topped jar with the lime juice and fish sauce. Set aside until needed.

To serve, thinly slice the beef and return it to the bowl it has been marinating in. Combine the cucumber salad with the fish sauce dressing and the ground chilli rice. Divide the salad leaves and the cucumber salad between plates and pile the sliced beef high on top to serve.

LAMB

One Tray Greek Lamb Mezze

There is no doubt that all the family will enjoy this healthy option, plus there is very little cleaning up as an added bonus. This one tray Greek lamb mezze not only cooks everything together in one roasting tin in the oven, but it can be brought straight to the table with a flourish.

250g (9oz) minced lamb

50g (2oz) fresh brown breadcrumbs

1 egg, beaten

½ tsp dried oregano

2 red onions, halved

2 tbsp chopped fresh flat-leaf parsley

2 large potatoes, cut into wedges

1 courgette, cut into batons

12 cherry tomatoes

2 tbsp olive oil

100g (4oz) feta cheese, crumbled

handful of good-quality pitted black olives, halved

sea salt and freshly ground black pepper

SERVES 4

Preheat the oven to 200°C (400°F/gas mark 6).

Place the lamb, breadcrumbs, egg, oregano and seasoning in a bowl, then grate in half an onion and add 1 tablespoon of the parsley. Using your hands, mix until well combined and shape into eight even-sized patties. Place in a large, shallow roasting tin.

Cut the rest of the onion halves into wedges and arrange them around the lamb patties with the potato wedges, courgette batons and cherry tomatoes. Drizzle over the olive oil and season to taste.

Roast for about 40 minutes, turning everything once, until the lamb patties are cooked through and the vegetables are all tender and lightly charred.

Remove the tin from the oven and scatter over the feta cheese and black olives with the rest of the parsley. Bring straight to the table to allow everyone to help themselves.

Lamb Fillet with Blue Cheese and Mint Dressing

This lamb salad is packed full of strong flavours. Don't be tempted to overcook the lamb – it's best served rare. This would be lovely served with couscous or tricolour quinoa, but it should be satisfying served just as it is.

4 x 150g (5oz) lamb fillets, well trimmed and any excess fat removed

1 tbsp rapeseed oil

50g (2oz) button mushrooms, thinly sliced

100g (4oz) French green beans, trimmed

100g (4oz) green baby salad leaves, such as baby spinach and rocket

8 cherry tomatoes, halved

50g (5oz) Cashel Blue or Bellingham Blue cheese, crumbled

50g (2oz) toasted flaked almonds

DRESSING:

2 tbsp crème fraîche

1 tsp clear honey

50g (5oz) Cashel Blue or Bellingham Blue cheese, crumbled

2 tbsp olive oil

1 tsp sherry vinegar

1 tsp chopped fresh mint

sea salt and freshly ground black pepper

SERVES 4

Heat a large frying pan over a high heat until it's searing hot. Season the lamb fillets with salt and pepper. Add the oil to the heated pan, then add the lamb fillets. Reduce the heat to a medium to high heat and cook for 5–6 minutes, turning regularly, until just cooked through and tender but still pink in the middle. Leave to rest for 5–10 minutes, covered loosely with foil to keep warm.

Meanwhile, add the mushrooms to the pan you cooked the lamb fillets in. Season to taste and sauté on a medium to high heat for 2–3 minutes, until cooked through and tender.

Blanch the green beans in a pan of boiling salted water for 3–4 minutes, until just tender. Drain and quickly refresh under cold running water. Drain and dry well on kitchen paper.

For the dressing, place the crème fraîche and honey in a small pan. Gently warm through, then remove from the heat and add the blue cheese. Whisk until the cheese has melted into the crème fraîche, then whisk in the olive oil, vinegar and mint. Season to taste.

Place the salad leaves in a bowl and add the tomatoes, crumbled blue cheese, cooked mushrooms and blanched green beans.

Carve each rested lamb fillet into thin slices. Divide the salad between four plates and arrange the lamb slices on top, then drizzle over the warm dressing and scatter over the toasted flaked almonds to serve.

Moroccan Spiced Lamb Koftas with Chunky Salad and Pitta

These spicy little nuggets of minced lamb would also be delicious cooked on the barbecue if the weather is right. Serve everything on a large board for maximum impact, then pop in the middle of the table with a pile of plates and allow everyone to help themselves.

KOFTAS:

450g (1lb) lean lamb mince

1 small red onion, grated

2 garlic cloves, crushed

1 tbsp chopped fresh coriander

1 tbsp harissa paste

1 tsp freshly grated root ginger

¼ tsp ground cumin

¼ tsp ground coriander

¼ tsp ground turmeric

¼ tsp sweet paprika

1 tbsp olive oil

SALAD:

1 small head of iceberg lettuce, cut into wedges

1 small red onion, grated

1 baby cucumber, grated and squeezed dry

100g (4oz) cherry tomatoes, cut into quarters

handful of pitted black olives, roughly chopped

50g (2oz) feta cheese

handful of fresh mint leaves, roughly torn

4 heaped tbsp natural yoghurt

1–2 tsp harissa paste

sea salt and freshly ground black pepper

4 wholemeal pitta breads

lemon wedges, to garnish

SERVES 4

To make the spiced lamb koftas, mix the lamb mince in a bowl with the onion, garlic, fresh coriander, harissa paste, ginger and spices and season with salt and pepper. Using slightly damp hands, divide into eight portions and shape into thick, fat sausage shapes.

Heat a large non-stick frying pan over a medium heat. Add the olive oil and cook the koftas for 10–12 minutes, until cooked through and golden brown, turning regularly with a tongs.

Arrange the wedges of iceberg lettuce on one end of a nice large board. Scatter over the grated red onion, grated cucumber, cherry tomatoes and olives. Crumble the feta on top and sprinkle over the mint. Mix the yoghurt with enough harissa to your liking and season with salt and pepper, then drizzle over the salad.

Toast the pitta breads under a preheated medium grill (or just use the toaster), then cut in half and arrange on the board with the spiced lamb koftas or on a separate platter. Garnish with the lemon wedges to serve.

Seared Lamb Fillet with Mediterranean Butter Bean Stew

This butter bean stew is packed full of gutsy flavours, but it all depends on making a good chunky tomato sauce. I find that whole peeled plum tomatoes in a can are a superior product and much better value than canned chopped tomatoes. I will also pay a little extra for a more authentic-looking Italian can and I haven't been disappointed yet!

4 x 150g (5oz) lamb fillets, well trimmed and any excess fat removed

1 tbsp extra virgin olive oil

1 large garlic clove, thinly sliced

pared rind of 1 lemon

handful of fresh rosemary sprigs

BUTTER BEAN STEW:

1 tbsp olive oil

1 large red onion, finely chopped

2 garlic cloves, finely chopped

1 tbsp chopped fresh sage

good pinch of dried chilli flakes

150ml (¼ pint) chicken stock

1 x 400g (14oz) can of good-quality whole plum tomatoes

1 tbsp red wine vinegar

pinch of dried oregano

2 x 400g (14oz) cans of butter beans, drained and rinsed

50g (2oz) feta cheese

1 tbsp roughly chopped fresh flat-leaf parsley

sea salt and freshly ground black pepper

SERVES 4

Rub the lamb fillets with the olive oil and garlic. Season well and pare over the lemon rind, then add the rosemary, mixing well to combine. Set aside at room temperature while you prepare the beans, or overnight in the fridge, covered with cling film, is fine too.

To make the butter bean stew, heat the olive oil in a sauté pan over a medium heat. Tip in the onion, garlic, sage and chilli flakes and sauté for about 5 minutes, until softened. Pour in the stock and allow it to bubble down, stirring. Then add the tomatoes, crushing them up with your hands, along with the red wine vinegar and oregano and season with salt and pepper to taste. Bring to the boil, stirring, then reduce the heat and stir in the beans. Simmer for about 15 minutes, until most of the excess liquid has evaporated.

Meanwhile, put a large non-stick frying pan over a high heat until it's very hot. Brush the marinade ingredients off the lamb fillets, then add to the pan. Reduce the heat a little to a medium to high heat and quickly sear for 5–6 minutes, turning regularly, until just cooked through and tender but still pink in the middle. Leave to rest in a warm place for about 10 minutes.

Spoon the butter bean stew into wide-rimmed bowls, then carve the lamb fillets into thick slices and arrange on top. Crumble over the feta and scatter the parsley on top to serve.

Chargrilled Lamb Chops with Lemon and Herb Quinoa

This is a great dish to get ahead on the night before you want to eat it, and then you've very little to do to get a delicious meal on the table. You could also serve this quinoa with a simple piece of grilled fish or chicken.

1 tbsp cumin seeds

1 large garlic clove, peeled

good pinch of dried chilli flakes

finely grated rind and juice of 1 lemon

3 tbsp extra virgin olive oil

8 lamb chops, well trimmed

250g (9oz) quinoa

500ml (18fl oz) water

1 bunch of spring onions, trimmed and thinly sliced

3 tbsp chopped fresh coriander

1 tbsp chopped fresh mint

sea salt and freshly ground black pepper

steamed long-stemmed or purple sprouting broccoli, to serve

SERVES 4

Toast the cumin seeds in a small pan over a medium heat just until fragrant, then tip into a pestle and mortar. Add the garlic, chilli flakes and lemon rind and season with salt and pepper. Bash everything together, then whisk in the lemon juice and olive oil.

Put the lamb chops into a shallow, non-metallic dish and rub over half of the cumin mixture. Set aside at room temperature while you prepare the quinoa, or overnight in the fridge, covered with cling film, is fine too.

Rinse the quinoa in cold water and then place in a pan with the water. Put on a medium heat and bring to the boil, then reduce the heat slightly and boil gently for 10 minutes. Turn the heat off, then stir through the rest of the cumin mixture. Cover tightly with cling film and leave for another 10 minutes (or longer is fine).

Meanwhile, heat a griddle pan over a high heat until it's smoking hot. Add the marinated lamb chops and cook for 3–4 minutes on each side, until cooked to your liking. Remove from the heat and leave to rest for at least 5 minutes.

When ready to serve, fluff up the quinoa with a fork, then stir in the spring onions, coriander and mint and divide among four plates. Add the chargrilled lamb chops and some steamed broccoli.

VEGETARIAN

Roasted Aubergines with Cherry Tomatoes and Goat's Cheese

It's not without reason that in the Middle East and throughout Italy, aubergines are still regarded as the poor man's meat. Good aubergines should be light in weight and not have too many seeds inside, and they should have a tight, shiny skin. They make an excellent vegetarian main course or light lunch, as they are so rich in nutrients. Prepare this in advance and simply pop in the oven just before you're ready to serve.

2 large aubergines

3 tbsp olive oil

1 red pepper

1 shallot, finely chopped

small handful of fresh basil leaves, torn

225g (8oz) cherry tomatoes, halved

2 x 100g (4oz) individual goat's cheeses (with rind), thinly sliced

sea salt and freshly ground black pepper

lightly dressed green salad, to serve

SERVES 4

Preheat the oven to 200°C (400°F/gas mark 6).

Cut the aubergines in half and trim off the stalks. Brush the cut sides with a little of the oil and season with salt and pepper, then place in a roasting tin with the red pepper and bake for 30–35 minutes, until the flesh of the aubergine is tender and the skin of the red pepper is blackened and blistered.

Meanwhile, heat a tablespoon of the oil in a frying pan set over a medium heat and sauté the shallot for 2–3 minutes, until softened but not browned. Set aside.

Remove the roasted vegetables from the oven (leave the oven turned on), and once the red pepper is cool, peel away the skin and finely chop the flesh, discarding the seeds. Place in a bowl with the sautéed shallot. Scoop out the flesh from the aubergines to within 1cm (1/2in) of the skin and finely chop the removed flesh. Add to the red pepper and shallot mixture, then add the basil and season generously with salt and pepper.

Pile the mixture back into the aubergine shells and arrange the cherry tomatoes and slices of goat's cheese on top. Drizzle over the remaining oil and return to the oven for 20–25 minutes, until the cherry tomatoes are lightly charred and the goat's cheese is bubbling. Arrange on plates with the lightly dressed salad to serve.

Porcini and Artichoke Pasta

Although porcini mushrooms are expensive, just a small amount added to a recipe will make an enormous difference to the flavour. They are intensely savoury and concentrated in this delicious pasta dish. I've used the oil from the artichokes as an element of the sauce.

25g (1oz) dried porcini mushrooms

1 x 275g (10oz) jar of artichoke hearts preserved in olive oil, drained and cut in half (oil reserved)

1 onion, diced

2 garlic cloves, crushed

1 tsp chopped fresh thyme

150ml (¼ pint) dry white wine

finely grated rind and juice of 1 lemon

350g (12oz) linguine pasta

50g (2oz) wild rocket

2 tbsp roughly chopped fresh flat-leaf parsley

50g (2oz) freshly grated Parmesan, plus extra shavings to garnish

sea salt and freshly ground black pepper

SERVES 4

Place the porcini mushrooms in a small bowl and pour over enough hot water to cover them. Leave to stand for 20 minutes to rehydrate.

Heat 2 tablespoons of the reserved oil from the artichokes in a heavy-based pan. Tip in the onion and garlic and sauté for about 3 minutes, until softened but not browned. Stir in the thyme, then pour in the wine and lemon juice and cook for 5 minutes, stirring occasionally, until slightly reduced.

Drain the porcini mushrooms, reserving the liquid, and finely chop. Add to the wine mixture with the reserved soaking liquid and simmer for about 5 minutes, until reduced by half.

Meanwhile, cook the linguine in a large pan of boiling salted water for 10–12 minutes, until al dente, or according to the packet instructions.

Add a little more of the reserved artichoke oil into the reduced porcini mixture, then fold in the artichoke hearts. Allow to warm through, then stir in the rocket, parsley and lemon rind and cook for another 30 seconds or so, until the rocket is just wilted. Season to taste.

Drain the pasta and shake well to remove any excess water, then return it to the pan and stir in the porcini and artichoke sauce and the Parmesan. Divide among warmed wide-rimmed bowls and scatter over a little extra Parmesan to serve.

Crispy Spinach and Feta Filo Pie

This is a great vegetarian option that should suit all the family. Traditionally known as spanakopita, which are normally bite-sized pastries, this pie is much less fiddly and is easier to make. It can be made up to a day in advance and kept covered in the fridge.

4 tbsp olive oil

1 onion, finely chopped

4 spring onions, finely chopped

300g (11oz) baby spinach

225g (8oz) feta cheese

2 large eggs

25g (1oz) freshly grated Parmesan cheese

2 tbsp chopped fresh mint

good pinch of freshly grated nutmeg

6 sheets of filo pastry, thawed if frozen

sea salt and freshly ground black pepper

cherry tomato, red onion and basil salad, to serve

SERVES 4–6

Preheat the oven to 180°C (350°F/gas mark 4).

Heat 1 tablespoon of the oil in a pan over a medium heat and add the onion. Sauté for a couple of minutes, until softened but not browned. Stir in the spring onions and cook for another minute. Add the spinach a handful at a time until it has all wilted down. Tip into a colander and press out any excess liquid, then cool.

Crumble the feta cheese into a large bowl and lightly mash with a fork. Mix in the cooled spinach mixture, eggs, Parmesan, mint and nutmeg. Season to taste.

Unroll the filo pastry and brush a 20cm (8in) clip-sided or loose-based tin with a little of the oil. Lightly brush each sheet with a little of the oil and place in the tin, oiled side down, leaving the excess hanging over the edge. Rotate the tin a quarter turn after putting in each sheet.

Tip the filling into the tin and fold the excess pastry over the top one sheet at a time to give a ruffled effect. Brush any remaining oil on top.

Bake for about 45 minutes, until crisp and golden brown. Remove from the oven and leave to settle for 5 minutes.

Take the spinach and feta pie out of the tin and cut into slices. Arrange on plates with the cherry tomato, red onion and basil salad to serve.

Spicy Roasted Root Vegetables with Lemon and Herb Couscous

Couscous is a staple of the North African diet and can be used to accompany tagines or with great success in salads. It's made from semolina grains that have been rolled, dampened and coated with very fine wheat flour. This enlarges the individual grains and keeps them separate during cooking.

COUSCOUS:

225g (8oz) couscous

450ml (¾ pint) vegetable stock

2 tbsp olive oil

1 small red onion, finely diced

1 garlic clove, finely chopped

finely grated rind of 1 lemon

2 tbsp chopped fresh mixed herbs, such as parsley, basil and coriander

ROOT VEGETABLES:

2 tbsp olive oil

500g (1lb 2oz) baby carrots, trimmed and halved lengthways

500g (1lb 2oz) baby parsnips, trimmed and halved lengthways

2 tbsp light soy sauce

1 tbsp clear honey

1 mild red chilli, seeded and finely chopped

2 tbsp chopped fresh flat-leaf parsley

1 tsp toasted sesame seeds

sea salt and freshly ground black pepper

SERVES 4

Preheat the oven to 180°C (350°F/gas mark 4).

To prepare the spicy roasted root vegetables, place the oil in a large roasting tin and add the carrots and parsnips, tossing until well coated. Season generously. Roast for 15 minutes, until almost tender.

Meanwhile, place the couscous in a large heatproof bowl. Bring the stock to a simmer and then pour it over the couscous. Stir well, then cover with cling film and set aside for 15 minutes.

Remove the root vegetables from the oven, then drizzle over the soy sauce and honey and sprinkle the red chilli on top, tossing to coat evenly. Return to the oven and roast for another 10 minutes, until the vegetables are completely tender and lightly charred. Sprinkle over the parsley and sesame seeds and toss gently until evenly coated.

To finish the couscous, heat a frying pan with the olive oil. Sauté the onion, garlic and lemon rind for 2-3 minutes, until softened but not browned. Remove from the heat.

Gently separate the couscous grains with a fork. Season to taste and place in a pan to reheat, stirring continuously with a fork. Fold in the onion mixture along with the herbs.

To serve, divide the couscous among warmed bowls and arrange the spicy roasted root vegetables on plates alongside.

Griddled Halloumi with Red Onion, Haricot Bean and Tomato Salad

I first enjoyed halloumi while on holiday in Cyprus, where it has been produced for centuries. It's a semi-hard cheese prepared from the milk of sheep, cows or goats and then sometimes rolled in wild mint. It has a distinct and pleasant flavour and is versatile to cook with, as its springy texture always retains its shape even when fried or griddled. This dish would serve two as a main or four as a starter or light lunch.

250g (9oz) halloumi cheese
½ tsp sweet or smoked paprika
1 tbsp olive oil
juice of ½ lemon
2 wholewheat pitta breads

SALAD:

1 garlic clove, crushed
finely grated rind and juice of ½ lemon
1 tbsp extra virgin olive oil
1 x 400g (14oz) can of haricot beans, drained and rinsed
1 small red onion, diced
12 vine-ripened cherry tomatoes, halved
12 pitted black olives, halved
1 tsp chopped fresh flat-leaf parsley
small handful of fresh mint leaves
sea salt and freshly ground black pepper

SERVES 2–4

To make the salad, place the garlic, lemon rind and juice and olive oil in a pan set over a low heat, stirring to combine. Fold in the haricot beans with the red onion, tomatoes, olives and herbs and season with salt and pepper to taste, then leave to warm gently for 5 minutes. Remove from the heat and place in a bowl to marinate at room temperature for 1 hour to allow the flavours to develop.

When ready to cook, heat a griddle pan and a frying pan over a medium to high heat. Cut the halloumi cheese into six thick slices and dip them into cold water, then dust with the paprika. Spray the griddle pan with the olive oil and add the halloumi cheese. Fry for 4 minutes, turning once, until lightly charred and golden. Remove from the heat and squeeze the lemon juice over the cheese.

Meanwhile, arrange the pittas on the frying pan and cook for 1 minute, turning once, until puffed up. Alternatively, put the pittas in a toaster for a minute or two. Cut into slices on the diagonal.

Spoon the red onion, haricot bean and tomato salad into the centre of plates and arrange the grilled halloumi on top, spooning over the lemon-flavoured pan juices. Arrange the slices of griddled pitta bread around the salad to serve.

EGGS

Egg and Cauliflower Curry

I like to serve this curry with some wholewheat chapatis, which are great for scooping up the sauce. They are now stocked in a number of the larger supermarkets or you'll find them in any ethnic food store, otherwise it's also delicious with rice.

2 tbsp rapeseed oil

1 tsp cumin seeds

½ cinnamon stick

2 whole cloves

1 bay leaf

1 large onion, very finely chopped

2 garlic cloves, finely chopped

2 x 400g (14oz) cans of chopped tomatoes

2 green chillies, seeded and finely chopped

2 handfuls of fresh coriander, chopped, plus extra leaves to garnish

1 tbsp freshly grated root ginger

2 tsp ground turmeric

1 tsp garam masala

1 tsp tandoori curry paste or powder

1 tsp salt

good pinch of palm sugar

1 cauliflower, trimmed and cut into small florets

8 eggs (preferably free-range)

drop of white wine vinegar

shop-bought chapatis or basmati rice, to serve (optional)

SERVES 4-6

Heat the oil in a large pan and tip in the cumin seeds, cinnamon stick, cloves and bay leaf. When they are sizzling, add the onion and garlic. Reduce the heat to very low and cook gently for 5 minutes, stirring continuously. Cover and cook for another 5 minutes, then using a tongs, remove the cinnamon stick, cloves and bay leaf.

Increase the heat and sauté the onion until golden, pressing it against the sides of the pan to crush it down. Turn the heat down and add the tomatoes, chillies, coriander, ginger, turmeric, garam masala, tandoori paste or powder, salt and palm sugar, stirring to combine. Add the cauliflower, then bring to the boil, cover, reduce the heat again and simmer for another 10–15 minutes, or until the cauliflower florets are soft.

Meanwhile, hard-boil the eggs in a large pan of boiling water with the vinegar for about 7 minutes. Drain and rinse under cold running water to prevent them from cooking further. Shell the eggs and cut each one in half lengthways with a sharp knife. Nestle them on top of the cauliflower curry with the yolks facing upwards. Replace the lid and cook on a very low heat for another 10 minutes.

Divide among bowls and garnish with the coriander leaves, then serve with the chapatis or rice, if liked.

Smoked Haddock Hash with Poached Eggs

This brunch-worthy dish was inspired by the wonderful natural smoked haddock that has now become so widely available. It would also make a delicious light supper that will satisfy the most discerning guests.

1 tbsp white wine vinegar

4 large eggs (preferably free-range)

300ml (½ pint) milk

1 onion, finely sliced

1 bay leaf

4 x 100g (4oz) natural smoked haddock fillets, pin-boned

1 tsp prepared English mustard

squeeze of lemon juice

2 tsp cornflour mixed with 1 tsp water

1 tbsp snipped fresh chives

75g (3oz) watercress sprigs

HASH POTATOES:

450g (1lb) starchy potatoes (such as Russets), peeled and grated

25g (1oz) butter, melted

1 tbsp chopped fresh flat-leaf parsley

about 1 tsp olive oil spray

sea salt and freshly ground black pepper

SERVES 4

Place a large pan of water on a high heat. Add the vinegar and a pinch of salt. Bring to a rapid boil, then reduce the heat to a simmer, whisk the water and crack in two of the eggs. Cook for 3 minutes, until the eggs are just poached and holding their shape. Remove with a slotted spoon and put straight into a bowl of iced water. Repeat with the remaining two eggs. These eggs will keep happily in the fridge for up to two days.

Meanwhile, pour the milk into a large frying pan and add the sliced onion and bay leaf. Bring to a simmer over a medium heat, then carefully place the haddock into the milk, skin side down. Simmer for 2 minutes, then turn over and simmer for another 2 minutes, until the smoked haddock is just cooked through and tender. Lift the haddock out of the milk. Carefully remove and discard the skin and keep the haddock warm.

Strain the poaching milk through a sieve into a small clean pan to remove the onion and bay leaf. Put over a medium heat and whisk in the mustard and lemon juice and the cornflour mixture. Bring to the boil to thicken, whisking continuously. Season to taste, remove from the heat and keep warm, whisking in the chopped chives at the last minute.

Place the grated potatoes, melted butter, parsley and seasoning in a bowl and mix well. Heat a large non-stick frying pan over a medium to low heat and spray the base with olive oil. Place large spoonfuls of the mixture into the pan, flatten with a fish slice and cook for 5–6 minutes on each side, until crisp and golden brown. You will need 12 in total, allowing three per serving. Spray the pan with olive oil for each batch.

Place the cooked poached eggs into a fresh pan of boiling water for 1 minute to reheat them.

To serve, place a stack of three hash potatoes on each plate. Add a small pile of watercress to each one, then add a piece of the cooked smoked haddock. Top with a poached egg and drizzle the sauce on top. Finish each one with a light grinding of black pepper and a sprig of watercress.

Irish Breakfast Omelette

I love to make this omelette after a hard workout in the gym. It's high in protein but low in fat and makes for a very tasty breakfast. Omit the pancetta if you're looking for a vegetarian option – it will still taste delicious!

2 tsp olive oil

25g (1oz) pancetta (smoked bacon lardons)

50g (2oz) button mushrooms, sliced

1 spring onion, thinly sliced

50g (2oz) baby spinach leaves

2 egg whites (preferably free-range)

1 egg (preferably free-range)

1 tbsp water

4 cherry tomatoes, cut into quarters (preferably vine-ripened)

sea salt and freshly ground black pepper

lightly dressed crisp green salad, to serve

SERVES 1

Heat a medium non-stick frying pan over a medium heat. Add 1 teaspoon of the oil and fry the pancetta for 1–2 minutes, until it has released its fat and become crispy. Add the mushrooms and spring onion and season with salt and pepper. Continue to sauté for 2–3 minutes, until tender. Fold in the spinach and allow it to just wilt down. Tip into a sieve set over a bowl to drain off any excess liquid and cover loosely with foil to keep warm.

Whisk the egg whites and the whole egg in a bowl with the tablespoon of water and season lightly with salt and pepper. Wipe out the frying pan and return it to a medium heat with the remaining teaspoon of oil. Add the egg white mixture, swirling to evenly cover the bottom of the pan. Cook for 1 1/2 –2 minutes, until just set. Using a rubber spatula, lift the omelette and allow the runny egg white mixture to flow underneath.

Remove the omelette from the heat and spoon the pancetta, mushroom and spinach mixture on one side and scatter the cherry tomatoes on top. Fold over and slide onto a plate. Add a small mound of salad alongside to serve.

Pancetta Baked Eggs

If you're trying to avoid bread, this recipe makes a lovely breakfast served with steamed asparagus. Pancetta is just Italian streaky bacon, which is naturally drier than the bacon we're used to and therefore is much easier to slice very thinly, making it a perfect option for this dish.

olive oil, for spraying

4 semi-sun-dried tomatoes, diced

4 fresh basil leaves, torn

4 large eggs (preferably free-range)

2 thin slices of pancetta, cut in half

4 tbsp crème fraîche

2 tbsp freshly grated Parmesan

sea salt and freshly ground black pepper

snipped fresh chives, to garnish

steamed asparagus, to serve

SERVES 4

Preheat the oven to 190°C (375°F/gas mark 5).

Spray 4 x 200ml (7fl oz) baking dishes with olive oil. Sprinkle the sun-dried tomatoes and basil into the bottom of each one, then crack in an egg and add a slice of pancetta. Add a spoonful of crème fraîche and scatter the Parmesan on top. Season with salt and pepper.

Arrange the baking dishes in a shallow roasting tin and pour in enough boiling water to come halfway up the side of each dish. Carefully place in the oven and bake for 15 minutes, until the eggs are set and the cheese is bubbling. Set each dish onto a plate and garnish with the chives. Serve with a separate plate of steamed asparagus.

Smoked Salmon and Watercress Crêpes

This is a great recipe for a foolproof crêpe or pancake batter, with plenty of tips on how to get them exactly right. Traditionally, people said you should leave the batter for 30 minutes to allow the starch in the flour to swell, but there's really no need to do that – unless, of course, it suits your timetable, in which case the batter will keep happily in the fridge for up to two days. Just give it a good stir before using.

200g (7oz) smoked salmon slices
150g (5oz) crème fraîche
100g (4oz) watercress, well picked over
lemon wedges, to serve

CRÊPES:
100g (4oz) plain flour
2 eggs (preferably free-range)
300ml (½ pint) semi-skimmed milk
1 tbsp olive oil, plus extra for frying
1 tbsp snipped fresh chives
finely grated rind of 1 lemon
sea salt and freshly ground black pepper

SERVES 4

To make the crêpes, sift the flour into a large bowl with a pinch of salt and make a well in the centre. Crack the eggs into the middle, then pour in about 4 tablespoons of milk and 1 tablespoon of oil. Start whisking from the centre, gradually drawing the flour into the eggs, milk and oil. Once all the flour has been incorporated, beat vigorously until you have a smooth, thick paste. Add a little more milk if it's too stiff to beat. Gradually pour in the rest of the milk and add the chives and lemon rind, then whisk to loosen the thick batter – you should end up with a batter the consistency of single cream, so you may not need all of the milk.

Heat a large non-stick frying pan over a medium heat, then wipe it with oiled kitchen paper. Ladle some batter into the pan, tilting the pan to move the mixture around for a thin, even layer. Quickly pour any excess batter back into the bowl. If the temperature is right, the pancake should turn golden underneath after about 30 seconds. Flip it over and cook for another 30 seconds. Continue with the rest of the batter, folding the crêpes into quarters and covering with foil to keep them warm. Repeat until all the batter has been used – it should make eight crêpes in total.

Place the plate of crêpes on the table with a separate plate of the smoked salmon, bowls of crème fraîche and watercress and a little dish of lemon wedges. Allow everyone to help themselves while the crêpes are still warm.

TAKEAWAY MY WAY

Seafood Paella

Traditionally paella is made in Spain on a Saturday or Sunday, and it's usually made by the men to give women a day off from cooking. Calasparra is a low-starch, short-grain rice, and when cooked it's fluffy with separate grains. It's supposed to be the best rice to use for paella because it can absorb heaps of liquid, so it bursts with flavour. I've actually found it here in Ireland in SuperValu. To increase the quantities and serve more people (although you will need a giant paella dish!), allow about 80g of rice per person. You can buy a paella dish in Spain, so pick one up the next time you're on holiday.

3 tbsp extra virgin olive oil

8 large Dublin Bay prawns, shell on

1 onion, finely chopped

3 garlic cloves, finely chopped

2 vine-ripened tomatoes, grated (skin discarded)

1 tsp sweet paprika

½ tsp hot smoked paprika (pimenton picante)

150g (5oz) baby squid, cleaned and cut into rings

200g (7oz) Spanish short-grain rice (Calasparra, La Bomba or paella rice)

about 750ml (1 ¼ pints) hot fish stock

good pinch of saffron strands, soaked in a little water

12 large live clams, cleaned

12 large live mussels, cleaned

sea salt and freshly ground black pepper

lemon wedges, to garnish

lightly dressed green salad, to serve

SERVES 4

Heat 1 tablespoon of the olive oil in a 25cm (10in) paella dish set over a medium heat, then add the whole prawns and sauté for 2–3 minutes. Remove the prawns from the pan and set aside.

Heat the remaining 2 tablespoons of olive oil in the paella dish, then tip in the onion and garlic and sauté for 2–3 minutes, until softened. Add the grated tomatoes and cook for another 3–4 minutes, until reduced and thickened. Tip in the sweet and hot smoked paprika and cook for another minute, stirring.

Add the squid and sauté for a minute or so, then stir in the rice and continue to stir to ensure it's all evenly coated. Pour in 400ml (14fl oz) of stock with the saffron and season with salt and pepper. Increase the heat and bring to the boil, then reduce the heat and simmer for 15 minutes, stirring occasionally to ensure the rice doesn't stick to the bottom of the pan. Add more stock as necessary.

Arrange the sautéed whole prawns on top of the dish along with the clams and mussels, pushing them down into the rice but otherwise not disturbing it. Cook for about 8 minutes. If the dish looks very dry before the rice has cooked completely, sprinkle over a little more hot stock, but bear in mind it shouldn't be soupy.

Cover the dish with foil and take off the heat. Leave to rest for 10 minutes, then garnish with lemon wedges and serve straight to the table with a bowl of salad.

Baked Fish and Chips

Who doesn't love fish and chips? This is a much healthier version that uses olive oil spray, which is now available in all supermarkets. It's a very clever way of using just a tiny amount of oil so that the breadcrumbs don't dry out but still turn a nice golden colour. Don't tell anyone how you've cooked this and see if they notice…

4 x 150g (5oz) hake fillets, pin-boned and skin removed

finely grated rind and juice of 1 lemon

900g (2lb) Maris Piper potatoes

2 tbsp rapeseed oil

25g (1oz) plain flour

1 egg

25g (1oz) panko (toasted dried breadcrumbs)

1 tbsp chopped fresh flat-leaf parsley

1 tsp sesame seeds

about 1 tsp olive oil spray

lemon wedges, to garnish

lightly dressed green salad, to serve

TARTARE SAUCE:

2 gherkins, finely chopped

3 tbsp low-fat mayonnaise

3 tbsp thick Greek yoghurt

1 tbsp chopped rinsed capers

1 tbsp chopped fresh flat-leaf parsley

1 tsp lemon juice

sea salt and freshly ground black pepper

SERVES 4

Place the hake in a shallow dish, then sprinkle over the lemon juice and leave to marinate for 30 minutes covered with cling film in the fridge.

To make the tartare sauce, mix all the ingredients together and season with salt and pepper. Place in a small bowl and cover with cling film, then chill until needed.

When ready to cook, preheat the oven to 200°C (400°F/ gas mark 6). Line a baking sheet with parchment paper.

Cut the potatoes into thick chips. Bring a pan of salted water to the boil and blanch the chips for 5 minutes. Drain and dry well on kitchen paper. Place the chips onto two baking sheets and toss in the rapeseed oil, then arrange in a single layer and season with a little salt.

Put the flour on a plate and season with salt and pepper. Lightly beat the egg and place in a shallow dish. Mix together the breadcrumbs, lemon rind, parsley and sesame seeds in a shallow dish. Dip each hake fillet into the seasoned flour, shaking off any excess, then dip in the egg. Finally, coat each fillet evenly in the flavoured breadcrumbs and place on the lined baking sheet. Lightly spray with the olive oil.

Put the chips into the oven and cook for 10 minutes. Place the coated fish fillets in the oven and cook for another 15–20 minutes, until the fish is cooked through and golden brown and the chips are nicely golden.

Divide the fish and chips between four plates and add a small dish of the tartare sauce to each one along with a lemon wedge. Serve with separate bowls of green salad.

Peppered Beef Burgers with Sweet Potato Wedges

This has to be the ultimate makeover for a takeaway that we all enjoy – burger and chips. I've used lean minced beef and added lots of extra flavours to enhance the meat. Sweet potatoes have a very low GI, so they are a good healthy option.

500g (1lb 2oz) lean minced beef

1 garlic clove, crushed

1 tbsp tomato purée

1 tbsp chopped fresh flat-leaf parsley

2 tsp Worcestershire sauce

1 tbsp cracked black peppercorns

olive oil spray, for cooking

4 wholemeal bread rolls, split in half

about 4 tbsp tomato relish
(preferably Ballymaloe)

Little Gem salad leaves

4 small tomatoes, sliced

handful of thinly sliced red onion rings

SWEET POTATO WEDGES:

500g (1lb 2oz) sweet potatoes,
peeled and cut into wedges

1 tbsp olive oil

sea salt and freshly ground black pepper

SERVES 4

Preheat the oven to 200°C (400°F/gas mark 6).

Arrange the sweet potatoes in a shallow baking tin and drizzle with the olive oil. Toss until evenly coated, then season with salt and roast for 25–30 minutes, until cooked through and lightly golden.

Meanwhile, place the minced beef in a bowl with the garlic, tomato purée, parsley and Worcestershire sauce. Season with salt and freshly ground black pepper and mix until well combined. Divide the mixture into four and shape into patties. Put the cracked black peppercorns on a plate and press them into the burgers.

Preheat a non-stick frying pan over a medium heat and lightly spray with olive oil. Cook the burgers for about 4 minutes on each side for medium, or until they are done to your liking.

Toast the bread rolls on a hot griddle pan. Put a spoonful of the tomato relish on the bottom halves, then add a Little Gem salad leaf to each one. Top with a burger and then arrange the sliced tomatoes and red onion on top. Cover with the burger bun tops and arrange on plates with the sweet potato wedges.

Pad Thai Stir-Fried Noodles with Pork

The best pad thai noodles I ever ate were sitting in a small rickety chair on a Bangkok pavement. The aroma of all the wonderful ingredients was sensational and the flavour just blew me away. Here's my version, which I promise is much more delicious than any you'll find in a takeaway.

175g (6oz) Thai flat rice noodles (preferably Thai Gold brand)

100g (4oz) roasted peanuts

juice of 2 limes

1 red bird's eye chilli, finely sliced

3 tbsp Thai fish sauce (nam pla)

2 tsp rice vinegar

2 tsp dark soy sauce

1 tsp shrimp paste (from a jar)

1 tsp palm sugar (optional)

2 tbsp rapeseed oil

350g (12oz) piece of pork fillet, well trimmed, halved and thinly sliced

2 eggs, beaten

2 shallots, finely sliced

2 garlic cloves, finely chopped

200g (7oz) beansprouts

4 spring onions, trimmed and thinly sliced

2 tbsp roughly chopped fresh coriander, plus extra sprigs to garnish

lime wedges, to serve

SERVES 4

Soak the noodles in a large bowl with enough boiling water to cover them for 15 minutes, until softened and pliable. Drain the noodles in a colander, then place in a pan of boiling water and simmer for 45 seconds, until tender, or according to the packet instructions. Drain well.

Meanwhile, blend the roasted peanuts in a mini blender or roughly grind using a pestle and mortar. Set aside.

Mix together the lime juice, chilli, fish sauce, rice vinegar, soy sauce, shrimp paste and the palm sugar, if using, in a small bowl and set aside.

Heat 1 tablespoon of the oil in a wok until very hot, then stir-fry the pork for about 5 minutes, until cooked through and just turning golden. Remove with a slotted spoon and cover loosely with foil to keep warm. Pour in the eggs and quickly swirl the wok so that the egg sticks to the sides in a thin, even layer. Leave for about 30 seconds, until the eggs are just set, then break into small pieces with a wooden spoon. Remove and set aside with the pork.

Wipe the wok with kitchen paper and return it to a medium heat, adding the remaining tablespoon of oil. Stir-fry the shallots and garlic for 2–3 minutes, until softened and just beginning to brown. Pour the lime juice mixture into the wok and simmer for 1–2 minutes, until it has reduced and thickened slightly.

Add the drained noodles, beansprouts, spring onions and coriander to the wok. Toss for 1 minute to wilt the beansprouts, then return the cooked pork and egg to the wok and toss everything to combine.

Serve the pad thai noodles in warmed bowls. Garnish with sprigs of coriander and place the lime wedges and a little bowl of the ground peanuts to one side.

Pulled Chicken Tacos

Chipotle paste is a Mexican chilli paste that is now becoming more widely available. I have found it under the Discovery brand in Irish supermarkets and Fallon & Byrne and Picado Mexican Pantry in Dublin also have it in stock. Harissa paste would make a good alternative if you have any difficulty finding it.

8 chicken thighs, skinned and trimmed of any big bits of fat

2 tbsp chipolte paste (see the introduction)

1 small red onion, grated

250ml (9fl oz) passata (Italian sieved tomatoes)

5 tbsp barbecue sauce

12 crisp taco shells

1 Little Gem lettuce, shredded

1 small, ripe avocado, peeled, stoned and diced

100g (4oz) cherry tomatoes, quartered

sea salt and freshly ground black pepper

1 lime, cut into wedges, to serve

fresh coriander leaves, to garnish

SERVES 4–6

Preheat the oven to 180°C (350°F/gas mark 4).

Rub the chicken thighs with 1 tablespoon of the chipotle paste and season with salt and pepper. Mix the remaining tablespoon of chipotle paste with the onion, passata and barbecue sauce. Place in a small baking tin and add the chicken thighs in a single layer. Cover tightly with foil and bake for 1 hour.

Increase the oven temperature to 200°C (400°F/gas mark 6). Remove the foil from the chicken and roast for another 20 minutes, until the chicken is meltingly tender and almost falling off the bone. When the chicken is really tender, use two forks to shred the meat into the sauce, discarding the bones.

Arrange the taco shells on a baking sheet and place in the oven for 2–3 minutes to crisp up.

To serve, put some shredded lettuce into each taco and top with the pulled chicken. Scatter over the avocado and cherry tomatoes and season with a little salt and pepper. Arrange on plates with the lime wedges and garnish with the coriander to serve.

OMEGA-3

Cauliflower and Hazelnut Salad

This salad can be eaten on its own or served with some roast chicken or fish. It's perfect for making and serving at a later stage, as the flavours only seem to improve. Just fold the spinach in at the last minute or the leaves will become bruised and won't give the same contrast of texture.

1 medium cauliflower, broken into small florets

2 tbsp olive oil

1 red onion, thinly sliced

50g (2oz) skinned hazelnuts

50g (2oz) baby spinach leaves

3 tbsp raisins

DRESSING:

2 tbsp olive oil

1 tbsp sherry vinegar

2 tsp maple syrup

good pinch of ground allspice

pinch of ground cinnamon

sea salt and freshly ground black pepper

SERVES 4

Preheat the oven to 200°C (400°F/gas mark 6).

Toss the cauliflower in the olive oil in a large baking tin, then season with salt and pepper and roast for 15 minutes. Stir in the red onion and continue roasting for another 15-20 minutes, until the cauliflower is crisp and parts of it have turned golden brown and the red onion is just beginning to catch and char. Set aside to cool.

Place the hazelnuts in a small baking tin and roast for 10-12 minutes, until golden brown. Leave to cool a little, then roughly chop.

To make the dressing, place the olive oil in a screw-topped jar with the sherry vinegar, maple syrup, allspice and cinnamon. Shake until emulsified, then season with salt and pepper.

Put the roasted cauliflower and red onion in a large bowl and fold in the spinach, raisins and hazelnuts. Drizzle over the dressing, tossing to coat, then season to taste. Arrange on plates to serve.

Smoked Trout and Prawn Salad with Avocado and Tomato Salsa

This is the perfect salad for a dinner party or al fresco summer lunch. It's actually very simple to prepare but looks quite special. Of course, it only tastes as good as your raw ingredients, so it's worth buying the best produce you can find.

2 tbsp crème fraîche

2 tsp snipped fresh chives

1 tsp horseradish sauce

350g (12oz) smoked trout

handful of mixed baby salad leaves or micro herbs

350g (12oz) cooked peeled tiger prawns

brown soda scones with walnuts and flaxseeds (page 174), to serve (optional)

SALSA:

2 vine-ripened tomatoes, finely chopped

1 firm, ripe avocado, peeled, stoned and finely chopped

1 tbsp extra virgin olive oil, plus extra for drizzling

½ tsp balsamic vinegar

sea salt and freshly ground black pepper

SERVES 4

Mix the crème fraîche in a small bowl with the chives and horseradish and season with salt and pepper. Cover with cling film and chill until needed.

For the avocado and tomato salsa, place the tomatoes and avocado in a bowl and dress with the olive oil and balsamic vinegar, then season with salt and pepper. Cover with cling film and set aside at room temperature for up to 20 minutes to allow the flavours to develop.

Arrange the smoked trout on plates and spoon over the salsa, then arrange the salad leaves or micro herbs on top. Add a dollop of the horseradish crème fraîche and place a few prawns on top. Serve with the brown soda scones, if liked.

Brown Soda Scones with Walnuts and Flaxseeds

These scones are wonderfully light and their nuttiness is enhanced by the walnuts and the scattering of flaxseeds on top. These are best eaten warm from the oven or at least on the day that they are baked.

rapeseed oil,
for greasing the baking sheet

225g (8oz) plain flour,
plus extra for dusting

1 tsp bread soda

1 tsp salt

225g (8oz) coarse wholemeal flour

50g (2oz) shelled walnuts,
finely chopped

375ml (13fl oz) buttermilk

1 egg yolk mixed with 1 tbsp water

2 tbsp flaxseeds

MAKES ABOUT 9

Preheat the oven to 200°C (400°F/gas mark 6). Oil a large baking sheet and dust with flour.

Sift the plain flour, bread soda and salt into a large bowl. Add the coarse wholemeal flour and walnuts, mixing well to combine. Make a well in the centre, pour in 275ml (9 ½ fl oz) of the buttermilk and mix well with a wooden spoon, adding the remaining buttermilk as needed to make a soft, moist dough. Be careful not to over mix or the finished scones may be a little tough.

Dust a clean work surface with flour, then turn out the dough and dust the top with a little extra flour too. Using a rolling pin, roll out the dough until it's 2.5cm (1in) thick, then cut or stamp out individual scones with a 6cm x 5cm (2 ½ in x 2in) rectangular cutter. Place on the oiled and floured baking sheet. Brush the tops with the egg wash, then scatter over the flaxseeds.

Bake for 20–25 minutes, until well-risen and golden brown. Serve warm or at least on the day that they have been made.

Spaghetti with Sardines

This is the kind of pasta dish I make when there is nothing much left in the fridge. It's very easy to prepare and relies mostly on store cupboard ingredients. It has the added bonus of being super healthy to boot!

350g (12oz) spaghetti

1 tbsp olive oil

1 small red onion, finely chopped

2 garlic cloves, finely chopped

1 mild red chilli, seeded and finely chopped

1 x 400g (14oz) can of whole plum tomatoes

1 x 120g (4 ½oz) can of skinless, boneless sardines in tomato sauce

100g (4oz) pitted black olives, roughly chopped

2 tbsp rinsed small capers

good handful of fresh flat-leaf parsley, roughly chopped, plus extra to garnish

sea salt and freshly ground black pepper

SERVES 4

Cook the spaghetti in a large pan of boiling salted water for 10-12 minutes or according to the packet instructions until just tender but still with a little bite.

Meanwhile, to make the sauce, heat the olive oil in a large pan over a medium heat and sauté the onion for a couple of minutes. Add the garlic and chilli and sauté for 1 minute, stirring. Add the tomatoes, crushing them up with your hands, and the sardines in their tomato sauce and cook for another 2-3 minutes, roughly breaking up the sardines with a wooden spoon. Add the olives to the sauce along with the capers and parsley.

Drain the pasta and shake it well to remove any excess water, then return to the pan. Tip in the sauce and quickly stir until the spaghetti is evenly coated. Season with pepper, then divide among bowls and scatter over the parsley and another good grinding of black pepper to garnish.

Crispy Salmon with Pomegranate and Watercress Couscous

This is a super-healthy dish packed full of omega-3. Sumac is made from the dried berries of a flowering plant that are ground to produce an acidic, reddish-purple powder that is very popular in the Middle East. You'll find it in places like Fallon & Byrne in Dublin or ask a good local deli if they stock it.

250g (9oz) couscous

2 tbsp extra virgin olive oil, plus a little extra, if liked

500ml (18fl oz) boiling water

75g (3oz) rice flour

1 tbsp sumac, plus extra to garnish

150g (5oz) organic salmon fillets, pin-boned and skinned

75g (3oz) toasted pumpkin seeds

2 tbsp flax seeds

finely grated rind of 1 lemon

2 large handfuls of watercress

1 small pomegranate, halved and seeds removed (skin discarded)

lemon wedges, to garnish

HARISSA YOGHURT:

2 heaped tbsp thick Greek yoghurt

2 tsp harissa paste

sea salt and freshly ground black pepper

SERVES 4

Place the couscous in a heatproof bowl and season well, then stir in 1 teaspoon of the oil. Pour over the boiling water, cover tightly with cling film and set aside.

Heat the rest of the olive oil in a large non-stick frying pan over a medium to high heat. Put the rice flour in a shallow dish with the sumac and season generously with salt and pepper. Dust the salmon in the flour mixture, shaking off any excess. Add to the heated oil in the frying pan and cook for 2–3 minutes on each side, until crisp and golden.

Meanwhile, fluff up the couscous with a fork, then fold in the pumpkin seeds and flaxseeds with the lemon rind. At the last moment, roughly chop the watercress and toss it through the couscous with the pomegranate seeds.

Mix the yoghurt and harissa together in a small bowl and season to taste. Cover with cling film and chill until needed.

Arrange the crispy salmon on plates and add an extra light sprinkling of sumac. Add a small mound of the couscous, then drizzle over a little extra olive oil, if liked. Garnish with lemon wedges and add a spoonful of the harissa yoghurt to serve.

WHEAT FREE

Fragrant Pork and Sweet Potato Thai Red Curry

Thai curries are quick and easy to prepare. There is absolutely no need to go to the trouble of making your own curry paste, as most supermarkets now sell authentic ready-made pastes. I like to serve this curry with Thai fragrant rice, which has a characteristically soft and slightly sticky texture.

3 tbsp Thai red curry paste

1 large pork fillet, trimmed, halved and thinly sliced

2 garlic cloves, crushed

1 tbsp finely grated fresh root ginger

500ml (18fl oz) chicken stock

1 x 400ml (14fl oz) can of coconut milk

4 kaffir lime leaves, halved

2 medium sweet potatoes, peeled and cubed

1 tbsp fresh lime juice

1 tbsp Thai fish sauce (nam pla)

1 tsp palm sugar

handful of fresh basil leaves

handful of fresh mint leaves

2 spring onions, trimmed and sliced

handful of fresh coriander leaves

steamed Thai fragrant rice, to serve

SERVES 4

Heat a large non-stick pan or wok over a medium heat. Add the curry paste and cook for 1 minute. Add the pork, garlic and ginger and sauté for 5 minutes. Stir in the stock, coconut milk and lime leaves and bring to the boil. Reduce the heat and simmer for 15 minutes.

Add the sweet potatoes to the coconut and pork mixture and continue to simmer for another 15 minutes, until the pork and sweet potatoes are cooked through and tender. Stir through the lime juice, fish sauce and palm sugar. Finally, stir in most of the basil and mint.

Spoon the curry into deep bowls and scatter the remaining basil, mint and coriander on top. Serve with separate small bowls of the steamed rice.

Mackerel with Braised Puy Lentils and Sherry Vinaigrette

Mackerel is an under-used fish that is in plentiful supply. Naturally rich in oil and low in saturated fat, it's full of vitamins and minerals and is an excellent source of essential omega-3 fats. The body needs a regular supply of omega-3, so try to eat oil-rich fish, like mackerel, salmon or trout, at least once a week.

200g (7oz) Puy lentils

2 tbsp finely chopped carrot

2 tbsp finely chopped onion

about 350ml (12fl oz) chicken stock

2 tsp tomato purée

1 tsp balsamic vinegar

1 tbsp rapeseed oil

4 medium mackerel fillets, skin left on and pin bones removed

1 tbsp snipped fresh chives

1 tbsp chopped fresh flat-leaf parsley

25g (1oz) wild rocket

SHERRY VINAIGRETTE:

2 tbsp extra virgin olive oil

1 tbsp good-quality sherry vinegar

½ tsp maple syrup

½ tsp wholegrain mustard

sea salt and freshly ground black pepper

SERVES 4

Rinse the lentils under plenty of cold running water. Place in a pan, cover with water and bring to the boil. Add a good pinch of salt and simmer for 20 minutes, until the lentils are just tender but still holding their shape.

Meanwhile, to make the sherry vinaigrette, place the olive oil, vinegar, maple syrup and mustard in a screw-topped jar. Season to taste and shake vigorously until emulsified. Set aside until needed.

Drain the cooked lentils, then return to the pan and place over a low heat. Add the carrot, onion and enough stock to cover the lentils. Cook for 8–10 minutes, until the lentils have absorbed all the stock and are tender. Stir in the tomato purée and balsamic vinegar, then season to taste and keep warm.

Heat the rapeseed oil in a non-stick frying pan and season the mackerel fillets. Using a small, sharp knife, make small incisions in the skin to prevent the fish from curling up. Put the fillets in the heated pan, skin side down, and cook for about 5 minutes in total, turning once, until the skin is crispy and the mackerel is cooked through.

Stir the chives and parsley into the Puy lentils, then heap them into the centre of warmed plates and arrange the mackerel fillets on top. Drizzle over the sherry vinaigrette and scatter the rocket over each one to serve.

Cumin Roasted Lamb with Pumpkin Mash

It's important to use very fresh spices in this recipe, not ones that have been opened for a couple of months and left lurking in the back of the cupboard. If you have the time, you'll get an even better flavour if you dry roast the cumin and coriander seeds and then pound them to a powder in a pestle and mortar.

2 x 400g (14oz) French-trimmed lamb racks

2 tsp extra virgin olive oil

1 tsp ground cumin

steamed long green beans, to serve

PUMPKIN MASH:

1kg (2 ¼lb) small whole pumpkin, peeled, seeded and chopped

500g (1lb 2oz) potatoes, peeled and chopped

3 tbsp crème fraîche

½ tsp ground cumin

½ tsp ground coriander

sea salt and freshly ground black pepper

SERVES 6

Preheat the oven to 190°C (375°F/gas mark 5).

Brush the lamb racks with the olive oil and rub the ground cumin all over, then season with salt and pepper. Place the lamb in a roasting tin and cook for 20–25 minutes for medium rare or leave in for longer until cooked to your liking. Remove from the oven and cover loosely with foil. Set aside in a warm place to rest for 15 minutes.

Meanwhile, make the pumpkin mash. Place the pumpkin and potatoes in a large pan of cold salted water over a high heat. Bring to the boil, then reduce the heat to low and simmer for 15–20 minutes, until tender. Drain and return to the pan. Put back on the heat for 1–2 minutes to dry out, then add the crème fraîche, cumin and coriander. Mash until smooth, then season to taste. Keep warm until needed.

Carve the lamb into individual cutlets. Divide the pumpkin mash onto plates and top with the lamb cutlets. Add some steamed green beans to each plate to serve.

Warm Steak Salad with Horseradish Mustard and Balsamic Vinegar

This salad is packed full of earthy raw root vegetables that are shredded to make them easier to digest. The easiest way to prepare them is to use a mandolin. I've used micro greens from My Organics to garnish this salad. My Organics are based in Monaghan and won the SuperValu Taste of Cavan Award in 2014 for their innovative products.

1 tbsp rapeseed oil

4 x 200g (7oz) striploin steaks, trimmed

150g (5oz) mixed salad leaves

1 large carrot, cut into thin strips

1 beetroot, peeled and cut into thin strips

1 red onion, thinly sliced

½ celeriac, peeled and cut into thin strips

micro greens, to garnish (optional)

edible flowers, to garnish (optional)

DRESSING:

1 garlic clove, crushed

2 tsp creamed horseradish

1 tsp Dijon mustard

2 tbsp extra virgin rapeseed oil

1 tsp balsamic vinegar

1 tsp chopped fresh coriander

4 tbsp beef stock

sea salt and freshly ground black pepper

SERVES 4

Remember to take your steaks out of the fridge at least 30 minutes before you intend to cook them to allow them to come back up to room temperature.

To make the dressing, place the garlic, horseradish and mustard in a bowl, then whisk in the extra virgin rapeseed oil and balsamic vinegar to form a dressing. Season to taste and add the coriander. Set aside until needed.

Heat the rapeseed oil in a large heavy-based frying pan over a medium heat. Season the steaks, add them to the heated pan and fry for 4 minutes on each side, turning once, for medium rare. Remove from the pan and transfer to a plate. Cover loosely with foil to keep warm and leave to rest for 10 minutes.

Add the beef stock to the frying pan that you've cooked the steaks in. Bring to the boil and reduce by half, scraping the bottom of the pan with a wooden spoon to remove any sediment. Whisk into the dressing.

Place the salad leaves and vegetables in a large bowl and lightly coat with the dressing. Divide among plates, then carve the steaks into thin slices and arrange on top. Drizzle over any remaining dressing and garnish with the micro greens and the edible flowers, if using, to serve.

Tomato and Red Pepper Broth with Borlotti Beans and Cavolo Nero

Cavolo nero is a loose-leafed cabbage originally from Tuscany in Italy. Although from the same family as the kale we are more familiar with, its leaves are very dark green, almost black, hence its name, which translates as 'black cabbage'. It's in season from July through to early October and has a pleasantly tangy, bitter flavour with a sweet aftertaste.

900g (2lb) ripe tomatoes

1 tbsp olive oil

200g (7oz) pancetta (smoked bacon lardons)

1 onion, diced

1 courgette, trimmed and diced

2 garlic cloves, crushed

½ tsp smoked paprika

2 roasted red peppers, diced (from a jar or can)

1 tbsp tomato purée

1.7 litres (3 pints) chicken stock

100g (4oz) crème fraîche

small handful of fresh basil leaves

1 x 400g (14oz) can·of borlotti beans, drained and rinsed

100g (4oz) cavolo nero (black cabbage), shredded

4 tsp basil pesto (good-quality shop-bought or homemade)

25g (1oz) Parmesan shavings

sea salt and freshly ground black pepper

SERVES 4–6

Cut a criss-cross at the bottom of each tomato and put into a bowl of boiling water for 1 minute. Drain the tomatoes, then peel off the skin when they're cool enough to handle. Cut each tomato into quarters and remove the seeds and cores.

Heat the olive oil in a large pan over a medium heat. Add the pancetta, onion, courgette and garlic and sauté for 5 minutes. Stir in the smoked paprika and cook for 1 minute, then add the tomatoes, red peppers and tomato purée and cook for another 5 minutes. Stir in the stock and season to taste. Bring to the boil, then reduce the heat to a simmer and cook for about 15 minutes, until slightly reduced and thickened. Stir in the crème fraîche and basil. Remove from the heat and blitz with a hand blender.

Return the soup back to a medium heat and stir in the borlotti beans and shredded cavolo nero. Bring back to the boil, then reduce the heat and simmer gently for 3 minutes, until the kale is tender. If you think the soup is too thick, add a little water.

Ladle into shallow wide-rimmed bowls and add a swirl of basil pesto to each one. Sprinkle over the Parmesan shavings to serve.

DAIRY FREE

Spicy Chicken Noodles with Mango

The older I get, the more I find myself looking for tasty options that are healthy and packed full of goodness. This dish is a perfect example. Not only is it dairy free, but it's perfect for eating al fresco, whether you decide to cook the chicken under the grill or on a barbecue. Raw tiger prawns would make a nice alternative to the chicken.

450g (1lb) skinless chicken fillets, cut into 2.5cm (1in) strips

100g (4oz) vermicelli rice noodles

1 red onion, thinly sliced

good handful of fresh coriander leaves

handful of fresh mint leaves

1 firm, ripe mango, peeled, stone discarded and cut into fine strips

75g (3oz) toasted cashew nuts, roughly chopped

MARINADE:

1 garlic clove, crushed

juice of ½ lime

2 tbsp rapeseed oil

2 tbsp torn fresh basil leaves

1 tbsp dark soy sauce

1 tbsp sweet chilli sauce

1 tsp mild curry powder

DRESSING:

2 tbsp dark soy sauce

2 tbsp extra virgin rapeseed oil

1 tbsp sweet chilli sauce

juice of 1 lime

SERVES 4

Place all the ingredients for the marinade in a non-metallic bowl and mix well to combine. Stir in the chicken and cover with cling film. Chill for at least 2 hours or overnight is perfect to allow the flavours to penetrate the chicken.

Place the vermicelli rice noodles in a bowl and cover with boiling water. Leave for about 5 minutes, until softened, or according to the packet instructions. Place the red onion slices in a bowl of iced water for 2–3 minutes. This will make them crisp and will tone down the flavour a little. Drain both and place in a large bowl. Roughly tear the herbs and add to the bowl with the mango and cashew nuts.

Preheat the grill to high. Place the chicken strips on a foil-lined grill rack and cook for 3–4 minutes on each side, turning once, until cooked through and tender.

Meanwhile, make the dressing. Place the soy sauce in a small bowl, then whisk in the extra virgin rapeseed oil, sweet chilli sauce and lime juice.

To serve, add the cooked chicken and the dressing to the noodles and toss until well combined, then divide among wide-rimmed bowls.

Griddled Salmon with Avocado and Sun-Dried Tomatoes

Well-produced organic salmon is perfect for this dish. As it is farmed in colder waters, it has a firmer flesh. Salmon tastes far better if eaten slightly underdone rather than overcooked, and in this recipe it should be served warm, not hot. I've served it here with avocado, which is packed full of nutritional goodness.

4 x 175g (6oz) skinless organic salmon fillets, pin bones removed

olive oil, for brushing

½ lemon, pips removed

2 firm, ripe avocados (preferably Hass)

12 sun-dried tomatoes in oil, drained and finely chopped

½ small red onion, very finely chopped

25g (1oz) wild rocket

1 tbsp snipped fresh chives

sea salt and freshly ground black pepper

SERVES 4 AS A STARTER

Heat a heavy-based griddle pan until it's smoking hot. Cut each salmon fillet into three pieces, then season and brush each one with a little olive oil. Arrange on the griddle pan, then reduce the heat and cook for 1–2 minutes on each side, until just cooked through and golden brown. Remove from the heat and add a squeeze of lemon juice.

Cut each avocado in half and remove the stone, then carefully peel away the skin. Cut into thick slices and arrange in the centre of each plate or bowl, then scatter over the sun-dried tomatoes, red onion and rocket and season to taste. Arrange three pieces of the salmon on each one and scatter over the chives to serve.

Garlic and Mustard Beef Skewers with Creamy Chive Drizzle

These beef skewers are a hassle-free dinner, as most of the preparation can be done in advance. When cooking beef it's best to bring the meat to room temperature first, so I always remove the marinated beef from the fridge 30 minutes before cooking.

600g (1lb 5oz) trimmed rump or sirloin steak, cut into strips

4 soft wholemeal flour wraps

lightly dressed rocket salad

MARINADE:

2 garlic cloves, crushed

1 tbsp rapeseed oil

1 tbsp red wine vinegar

1 tbsp wholegrain mustard

1 tbsp soy sauce

1 tbsp honey

1 tsp chopped fresh thyme

1 tsp smoked paprika

CREAMY CHIVE DRIZZLE:

120ml (4fl oz) plain soya yoghurt

1 garlic clove, crushed

1 tbsp snipped fresh chives

1 tsp Dijon mustard

sea salt and freshly ground black pepper

SERVES 4

Place all the marinade ingredients into a bowl and mix well to combine, then add the steak strips and toss to coat. Cover with cling film and place in the fridge for 1–2 hours, or overnight is fine.

Remove the marinated beef from the fridge about 30 minutes before you want to cook it. Heat a griddle pan over a high heat until it's smoking hot. Thread the beef onto 8 x 15cm (6in) metal skewers and cook in batches for 2–3 minutes on each side for medium rare, or until it's cooked to your liking. Transfer to a plate and keep warm while you cook the remainder.

To make the creamy chive drizzle, mix together the plain soya yoghurt, garlic, chives and mustard in a small bowl. Season with salt and pepper and set aside until needed.

Heat the wraps for about 20 seconds on each side in a hot, dry and frying pan. Half-fill with the rocket salad, then arrange the beef skewers on top. Drizzle over the creamy chive drizzle to serve.

Satay Prawn Sticks with Griddled Limes

These are so easy to prepare, yet so colourful and visually appetising. I like to serve them as I've been given them in Thailand, with a small ramekin of rice that has been lightly oiled so that the rice can be turned out onto the plate. They would be absolutely delicious done on the barbecue and would take no more than 1 minute to cook on each side over medium to hot coals.

13 sticks of lemongrass

3 limes

2 garlic cloves, finely chopped

120ml (4fl oz) coconut milk

6 tbsp light soy sauce

2 tsp palm sugar

24 raw, headless tiger prawns, tails intact – about 600g (1lb 5oz)

spring onion and red chilli curls, to serve

rapeseed oil, for brushing

steamed Thai fragrant rice, to serve

DIPPING SAUCE:

50ml (2fl oz) rice wine vinegar

1 tsp palm sugar

1 baby cucumber or a 5cm (2in) piece, seeded and finely chopped

1 bird's eye red chilli, seeded and finely chopped

2 tsp chopped roasted peanuts

SERVES 4

Remove the tough outer leaves from one stick of lemongrass and finely chop the centre core. Grate the rind from one of the limes and squeeze out the juice. Place both in a non-metallic dish and add the garlic, coconut milk, soy sauce and palm sugar. Mix well to combine, then add the prawns. Set aside to marinade for about 15 minutes (or up to 2 hours in the fridge is fine). Cut the remaining two limes into small wedges (you'll need 12 wedges).

To make the dipping sauce, whisk together the vinegar and palm sugar in a small bowl, then add in the cucumber and chilli. Transfer to small serving bowls and sprinkle over the peanuts.

To make spring onion and red chilli curls, cut the green parts of one or two spring onions into two or three segments, then slice lengthways as thinly as possible with a paring knife. Place in a bowl of ice water for a few minutes, until they start to curl up. Remove and set aside. Cut the red chilli in half lengthways and scrape out the seeds, then slice lengthways into very thin strips and place in the bowl of ice water until they start to curl up too.

To thread the skewers, push two marinated prawns onto each lemongrass stick and finish with a lime wedge. Alternatively, you could use 12 x 15cm (6in) metal skewers or bamboo skewers that have been soaked in cold water.

Preheat a griddle pan over a medium heat and brush lightly with oil. Arrange the prawn skewers on the griddle pan and cook for 1–2 minutes on each side, until just cooked through.

Arrange on plates with small bowls of the dipping sauce and the steamed Thai fragrant rice garnished with spring onion and red chilli curls.

Rosemary Roast Lamb Chops with Roasted Potatoes and Cherry Tomatoes

There are times when it's a real lifesaver to be able to cook everything in the one tin and serve it straight to the table. This is just that sort of dish. It should fill the kitchen with wonderful aromas while it's cooking.

3 tbsp olive oil

8 lamb chops

1kg (2 ¼lb) potatoes, scrubbed and cut into small chunks

8 garlic cloves, peeled

4 fresh rosemary sprigs

4 small bunches of cherry tomatoes on the vine, each about 50g (2oz)

2 tsp balsamic vinegar

sea salt and freshly ground black pepper

lightly dressed leafy green salad, to serve

SERVES 4

Preheat the oven to 220°C (450°F/gas mark 7).

Heat 1 ½ tablespoons of the olive oil in a flameproof roasting tin or shallow ovenproof casserole dish over a medium heat. Season the lamb chops with salt and pepper and sear in two batches for 2 minutes on each side. Transfer to a plate with a tongs and set aside.

Add the remaining 1 ½ tablespoons of the olive oil to the tin and put it back on a medium heat. Sauté the potatoes for 4–5 minutes, until they are just starting to brown. Remove from the heat and stir in the garlic and rosemary, then tuck in the seared lamb chops. Place in the oven for 15 minutes.

Put the bunches of cherry tomatoes on the vine on top of the lamb and potato mixture and season with salt and pepper. Drizzle over the balsamic vinegar and return to the oven for 5 minutes, until the tomato skins have just started to split.

Serve straight to the table with a separate bowl of salad and allow everyone to help themselves.

REFINED SUGAR FREE

Coconut Carrot Slices

If you're looking for a treat for afternoon tea, look no further than this crunchy-topped traybake that uses honey instead of sugar with excellent results. This will keep for up to three days if stored in an airtight container, so it's a good option for lunchboxes, particularly as it has no nuts in it.

250g (9oz) butter

150g (5oz) honey

3 large eggs

1 tsp vanilla extract

200g (7oz) self-raising flour, sieved

50g (2oz) desiccated coconut

good pinch of sea salt

225g (8oz) carrots, grated

2 tsp mixed spice

TOPPING:

75g (3oz) desiccated coconut

3 tbsp honey

MAKES ABOUT 15 SQUARES

Preheat the oven to 180°C (350°F/gas mark 4). Line a 20cm x 30cm (8in x 12in) baking tin with parchment paper.

Gently melt the butter in a large pan and then leave to cool for 5 minutes. Add the honey, eggs and vanilla extract, then beat until smooth with a wooden spoon. Stir in the flour, coconut and salt. Finally, fold in the carrots and mixed spice. Transfer to the lined tin and bake for 30 minutes.

Meanwhile, to make the topping, mix the coconut with the honey and smooth this over the cake. Return to the oven for another 10–12 minutes, until golden. It should have slightly shrunk away from the sides of the tin and be springy to the touch. Remove from the oven and leave to cool completely, then cut into squares and use as required.

Cinnamon French Toast with Berries and Lime Crème Fraîche

There are times when everyone needs to feel like they've had a treat. This is my version of French toast, which relies on the natural sweetness of the berries to elevate it into something special. This would be delicious served as a leisurely brunch at the weekend, perhaps after (or before) a long walk.

2 eggs

150ml (¼ pint) milk

1 tbsp maple syrup or honey, plus extra to serve

½ vanilla pod, split in half and seeds scraped out

¼ tsp ground cinnamon

4 slices of white bread

25g (1oz) butter

selection of fresh berries, such as raspberries, strawberries, blueberries and blackberries

tiny fresh mint sprigs, to decorate

LIME CRÈME FRAÎCHE:

100g (4oz) crème fraîche

½ vanilla pod, split in half and seeds scraped out

finely grated rind and juice of 1 lime

SERVES 4

To make the lime crème fraîche, mix the crème fraîche with the vanilla seeds, then stir in the lime rind and juice. Cover with cling film and chill until needed.

To make the cinnamon French toast, whisk the eggs in a shallow dish with the milk, maple syrup or honey, vanilla seeds and cinnamon until well combined. Dip the slices of bread, one at a time, in the egg mixture for 30 seconds on each side.

Melt a little knob of the butter in a large non-stick frying pan on a medium to high heat. Fry one or two slices of the soaked bread for 2–3 minutes, turning once, until golden brown and crisp. Drain on kitchen paper while you cook the remainder with the rest of the butter.

Arrange the cinnamon French toast on plates and top each one with a quenelle of the lime crème fraîche. Drizzle with a little more maple syrup or honey, then scatter over the berries and decorate with the mint sprigs.

Coconut, Mango and Lemon Rice Pudding

This rice pudding uses Arborio rice, which is normally a risotto rice used in savoury dishes. It's also used in Italy for a type of rice pudding, but this one uses coconut milk. When cooked, the rounded grains should be firm, creamy and slightly chewy.

150g (5oz) Arborio rice (risotto rice)

1 x 400ml (14fl oz) can of coconut milk

300ml (½ pint) milk

finely grated rind and juice of 1 lemon

1 vanilla pod, split in half and seeds scraped out

1 firm, ripe mango

1 tbsp honey or maple syrup (optional)

SERVES 4

Place the Arborio rice in a medium-sized, heavy-based pan over a medium heat with the coconut milk, regular milk, lemon rind and juice, and the vanilla seeds. Bring to the boil, then reduce the heat to medium, cover and cook for 25 minutes, until the rice is tender but still with a little bite, stirring regularly.

Meanwhile, peel the mango and cut the flesh into slices, discarding the stone. When the rice pudding is cooked, taste it – if you think it needs a bit more sweetness, stir in the honey or maple syrup. Ladle into shallow wide-rimmed bowls and serve warm with the mango slices on top.

Hotcakes with Mango and Banana Sauté

These nifty little hotcakes are as light as a feather and can be made in the time it takes to heat the frying pan! You could serve them with berries, but the mango and banana is a delicious combination. And because both fruits are naturally high in sugar, this only needs a drizzle of maple syrup or honey to make it into what seems like a very decadent dessert.

HOTCAKES:

150g (5oz) self-raising flour

¼ tsp baking powder

tiny pinch of sea salt

1 large egg

250ml (9fl oz) buttermilk

a little sunflower oil, for frying

natural yoghurt, to serve

MANGO AND BANANA SAUTÉ:

25g (1oz) butter

1 large, firm, ripe mango, peeled and cut into bite-sized pieces

2 large bananas, peeled and thickly sliced on the diagonal

1 tbsp maple syrup or honey

juice of 1 lime

SERVES 4

Put the flour, baking powder and salt into a bowl. Make a slight dip in the middle and crack in the egg, then add the buttermilk and mix until smooth with a fork or small balloon whisk.

Put a large non-stick frying pan over a medium heat. Add a little sunflower oil, removing any excess with kitchen paper. Spoon 3 tablespoonfuls of the batter into the heated pan and cook for 1–2 minutes, until little bubbles rise up to the top. Using a spatula, carefully flip over and cook for another minute or so, until golden on both sides.

When the hotcakes are done, transfer them to a plate and cover with foil to keep them warm. Wipe the pan with kitchen paper and add a little more sunflower oil. Continue to make hotcakes with the rest of the batter. You should make about 12 hotcakes.

Once all of the hotcakes have been made, wipe out the frying pan with kitchen paper and add the butter. Once the butter is melted and sizzling, tip in the mango and bananas, tossing to coat. Sauté for 2–3 minutes, until heated through and just beginning to caramelise. Drizzle over the maple syrup or honey and lime juice and continue tossing until evenly coated.

Arrange three hotcakes on each serving plate. Add a spoonful of yoghurt to each one and spoon over the mango and banana sauté to serve.

Apple and Pecan Muffins

These muffins can be wrapped and frozen successfully for up to one month. I've used maple syrup instead of sugar, and as there is so much natural sweetness from the sultanas and apples, they actually need very little – it works out at only 1 teaspoon per muffin, which isn't bad if you fancy giving yourself a little treat.

100g (4oz) wholemeal flour

100g (4oz) self-raising flour

1 tbsp baking powder

1 tsp mixed spice

25g (1oz) wheat bran

2 eating apples, cored and finely chopped

50g (2oz) sultanas

50g (2oz) pecan nuts, chopped

25g (1oz) rolled oats

100ml (3 ½ fl oz) sunflower oil

2 eggs, beaten

4 tbsp maple syrup or honey

2 tbsp natural yoghurt

1 tsp sesame seeds

MAKES 12

Preheat the oven to 200°C (400°F/gas mark 6). Line a 12-hole muffin tin with paper cases.

Sift the flours, baking powder and mixed spice into a bowl. Add the bran left in the sieve and the rest of the wheat bran and mix to combine.

Add the apples, sultanas, pecans and oats and mix lightly with a wooden spoon. Make a well in the centre, then add the oil, eggs and maple syrup and stir to mix. Add the yoghurt and stir lightly until just combined – don't over mix.

Spoon the batter into the lined muffin tin until each case is three-quarters full. Sprinkle sesame seeds over the top.

Bake for 16–18 minutes, until firm to the touch. Remove from the oven and cool slightly. Serve warm.

Fresh Fruit Ice Lollies

These are perfect for when your child is begging for an ice lolly but you'd prefer to give them a healthy option. They are all rather delicious and certainly good enough to tuck in to one yourself…

WATERMELON AND RASPBERRY

¼ watermelon

200g (7oz) raspberries

MAKES 4

Cut the flesh from the watermelon and remove the seeds. Place in a food processor or blender with the raspberries. Blend until smooth, then strain through a sieve into a large jug. Pour into ice lolly moulds and freeze for at least 4 hours. To remove ice lollies from moulds, dip them briefly into hot water to loosen the lollies. Use as required.

BLACKBERRY AND ORANGE

300g (11oz) blackberries

juice of 2 oranges or 6 tbsp good-quality apple juice

MAKES 4

Place the blackberries in a food processor or blender with the orange or apple juice. Blend until smooth, then press through a sieve into a large jug. Pour into ice lolly moulds, then freeze and use as described above.

TROPICAL MANGO

2 medium mangoes

juice of 2 limes

MAKES 4

Peel the mangos and cut the flesh off the stone. Place in a food processor or blender with the lime juice, then blitz until smooth. Transfer to a large jug and use to fill ice lolly moulds, then freeze and use as described above.

Peanut Butter and Banana French Toast Sandwiches

This is a great healthy snack that can beat the afternoon energy slump that children sometimes have after a long day at school. The banana offers quick carbs and the peanut butter has a little protein. Cooking them in coconut oil not only adds flavour, but it is easily absorbed into the body and has excellent antiviral properties.

4 eggs, lightly beaten

4 tbsp milk

8 slices of wholemeal bread

cold pressed coconut oil, for cooking

8 heaped tbsp crunchy peanut butter (no added sugar or salt)

2 ripe bananas, peeled and sliced

SERVES 4

Place the eggs and milk in a shallow dish and whisk to combine. Dip the slices of bread, one at a time, in the egg mixture for 30 seconds on each side.

Melt a little coconut oil in a large non-stick frying pan. Add the dipped slices of bread in batches and cook for 1–2 minutes on each side, until the French toast is golden brown.

When half of the French toast is cooked, spread over the peanut butter and arrange the banana slices on top. Cover with the remaining pieces of French toast and then cut each one in half. Arrange on plates to serve.

Quick Quesadillas with Cherry Tomato and Avocado Salsa

These quesadillas are a perfect lunch or mid-morning snack for all of the family to enjoy. They can be prepared up to one hour in advance, covered with cling film and kept at room temperature. Simply flash through the oven when you are ready to serve.

8 soft wholemeal flour wraps

2 tbsp olive oil

2 x 100g (4oz) balls of mozzarella cheese, drained and sliced

4 spring onions, thinly sliced

1 roasted red pepper, cut into thin strips (from a jar or can is fine)

SALSA:

225g (8oz) cherry tomatoes, quartered

1 firm, ripe avocado, peeled, stoned and chopped

2 spring onions, thinly sliced

juice of ½ lime

1 tbsp olive oil

sea salt and freshly ground black pepper

SERVES 4

To make the cherry tomato and avocado salsa, place the tomatoes in a non-metallic bowl with the avocado, spring onions, lime juice and olive oil, stirring until well combined. Season to taste and leave at room temperature to allow the flavours to develop.

Preheat the oven to 200°C (400°F/gas mark 6) and heat a griddle pan over a medium to high heat until it's very hot.

Brush one side of each wrap with a little of the olive oil. Place one wrap in the pan, oiled side down, and cook for 1 minute, until nicely marked, pressing down with a spatula. Repeat with the remaining wraps.

Arrange half of the wraps on baking sheets, marked side down. Arrange the mozzarella cheese on top, then scatter over the spring onions and red pepper. Season to taste. Cover with the remaining wraps, marked side up, and bake for about 5 minutes, until heated through and the cheese has melted. Allow to cool slightly, until they are easy to handle.

Cut each quesadilla into four wedges with a serrated knife, pizza cutter or kitchen scissors. Arrange on warmed plates with separate small bowls of the cherry tomato and avocado salsa to serve alongside.

Crispy Chicken Strips with Peanut Satay Sauce

Cornflakes make a great coating for chicken or fish and I often use them instead of breadcrumbs, especially when I'm also cooking for my twins, Connor and Lucia. Before cooking they can be frozen, and once they are solid they can be stored in polythene bags. They are great finger food and you'll find that most children will enjoy them.

50g (2oz) plain flour

2 eggs

2 tbsp milk

150g (5oz) cornflakes, crushed

3 small boneless, skinless chicken breast fillets, cut into 8 even-sized strips

olive oil spray, for cooking

½ cucumber, cut into chunks

SATAY SAUCE:

2 tbsp crunchy peanut butter (no added salt or sugar)

2 tsp dark soy sauce

1 tsp palm sugar

juice of ½ lime

120ml (4fl oz) coconut milk

SERVES 4

To make the satay sauce, place the peanut butter in a small pan and stir in the soy sauce, palm sugar and lime juice. Gradually whisk in the coconut milk and heat gently for 2–3 minutes, until you have achieved a smooth sauce, then leave to cool.

Place the flour on a plate and season to taste. Beat together the eggs and milk in a separate dish. Put the crushed cornflakes in another dish. Toss the chicken strips lightly in the flour, then dip in the beaten egg mixture and finally coat with the cornflakes.

Spray a thin film of olive oil in a heavy-based frying pan and place over a medium heat. Sauté the coated chicken strips for 2–3 minutes on each side, until cooked through and tender. Drain briefly on kitchen paper.

Arrange the chicken strips on plates with small bowls of the satay dipping sauce and the chunks of cucumber to serve.

Healthy Anzac Biscuits

Anzac biscuits are traditionally made with rolled oats, butter, sugar, golden syrup, flour and coconut. I've adjusted the recipe to use wholegrain spelt flour, which is an ancient relative of modern wheat – the spelt grain has been around since Roman times. If you want to be super healthy, replace the butter with cold pressed coconut oil or macadamia nut oil. I buy coconut sugar in my local health food shop, but if you have difficulty finding it, replace it with light muscovado sugar.

100g (4oz) wholemeal spelt flour

150g (5oz) coconut sugar

100g (4oz) rolled oats

75g (3oz) desiccated coconut

125g (4 ½oz) butter, cold pressed coconut oil or macadamia nut oil

3 tbsp clear honey

½ tsp vanilla extract

pinch of bicarbonate of soda

1 tbsp warm water

MAKES ABOUT 20 BISCUITS

Preheat the oven to 180°C (350°F/gas mark 4). Line two large baking sheets with parchment paper.

Place the wholemeal spelt flour in a large bowl with the coconut sugar, oats and desiccated coconut.

Put the butter or coconut oil or macadamia nut oil in a small pan with the honey and vanilla extract and warm through over a gentle heat, stirring to combine.

Mix the bicarbonate of soda with the warm water in a small bowl to dissolve. Stir it into the butter mixture and mix well until it foams up a little in the pan. Remove from the heat and mix into the dry ingredients. Mix well to combine.

Spoon tablespoons of the biscuit dough onto the lined baking sheets. Bake for 6–8 minutes, until crisp and golden. Leave on the baking sheets for 5 minutes, then transfer to a wire rack and allow to cool completely. Store in an airtight tin for up to one week and use as required.

DESSERTS

Caramel Pear Tart

This tart has no refined sugar, using coconut sugar and maple syrup as sweeteners instead. Coconut sugar has been used in South-East Asian cookery for thousands of years and is now becoming widely available.

4 small, firm, ripe pears, peeled, halved and cored

2 tbsp pure apple juice

crème fraîche, to serve

FILLING:

150g (5oz) maple syrup

40g (1 ½oz) butter, melted

3 eggs

1 vanilla pod, split in half and seeds scraped out

8 tbsp coconut sugar

3 tbsp almond milk

VANILLA PASTRY:

175g (6oz) plain flour

150g (5oz) cold butter, diced, plus extra for greasing

50g (2oz) coconut sugar

1 egg yolk

1 vanilla pod, split in half and seeds scraped out

½ tsp almond milk

1 egg white, lightly beaten, for brushing

SERVES 6–8

First make the vanilla pastry. Place the flour, butter, coconut sugar, egg yolk, vanilla seeds and almond milk in a food processor and process briefly to combine. Wrap in cling film and leave to rest in the fridge for 1 hour.

Preheat the oven to 180°C (350°F/gas mark 4).

Place the pears and apple juice in a large frying pan over a medium heat. Cover with a lid and cook for 8 minutes, until the pears are tender when pierced with the tip of a sharp knife. Set aside and leave to cool.

Roll out the rested vanilla pastry until it's 3mm ($1/4$ in) thick, then use to line a lightly greased loose-bottomed 28cm (11in) shallow tart tin. Trim away the excess pastry. Gently press the edges with a small knife and place on a baking sheet. Bake blind for 15 minutes, then brush with the egg white and return to the oven for another 2–4 minutes, until a nice glaze has formed.

Reduce the oven temperature to 160°C (325°F/gas mark 3).

To make the caramel filling, place the maple syrup, melted butter, eggs, vanilla seeds, coconut sugar and almond milk in a bowl and whisk to combine. Arrange the cooked pear halves on the base of the cooked pastry shell, cut side down, and carefully pour over the caramel filling.

Bake for 35–40 minutes, until just set. Allow to cool in the tin, then cut into slices and arrange on plates to serve with dollops of crème fraîche.

Sticky Orange Upside Down Cake

I like to serve this citrus cake with a dollop of thick Greek yoghurt, but if you are trying to reduce your dairy intake, coconut yoghurt would also be yummy. Spooning the orange syrup over the cake will help to keep it wonderfully moist for three or four days if it's kept covered with cling film and stored in the fridge.

4 eggs

200g (7oz) honey

1 vanilla pod, split in half and seeds scraped out

½ tsp ground cinnamon

150g (5oz) self-raising flour

150g (5oz) butter, melted

125g (4 ½oz) ground almonds

thick Greek yoghurt, to serve

STICKY ORANGE TOPPING:

150g (5oz) honey

4 whole star anise

1 vanilla pod, split in half and seeds scraped out

5 tbsp water

½ tsp freshly grated root ginger

1 orange, very thinly sliced (skin on and all pips removed)

SERVES 6–8

Preheat the oven to 160°C (325°F/gas mark 3).

To make the sticky orange topping, place the honey, star anise, vanilla seeds, water and grated ginger in a large ovenproof frying pan over a medium heat. Stir until the honey has dissolved, then add the orange slices and simmer for 10–15 minutes, until the orange slices are soft. Remove from the heat and set aside to cool down completely.

Lightly grease a 20cm (8in) springform cake tin and line the base with parchment paper. Arrange the orange slices in an even layer on the bottom and reserve any excess syrup to use later.

Place the eggs, honey, vanilla seeds and cinnamon in the bowl of a standalone electric mixer and whisk for 8–10 minutes, until the mixture is thick, pale and has tripled in volume. Sieve the flour over the egg mixture and gently fold it through, then fold through the melted butter and ground almonds.

Pour the batter over the orange slices and bake for 50 minutes, until the cake is cooked through when tested with a skewer. Allow to cook for 5 minutes, then invert the cake onto a platter, release the cake from the tin and spoon over the reserved orange syrup. Cut into slices and serve with dollops of yoghurt.

Coffee Cake with Mixed Toffee Nuts

A perfect dessert after a meal. This is very filling, so you'll find a little goes a long way. Use any nuts you fancy, mixed or otherwise – just make sure they are raw and haven't been salted.

150g (5oz) butter, softened, plus extra for greasing

100g (4oz) coconut sugar

1 tsp vanilla extract

1 egg

1 egg yolk

150g (5oz) plain flour, sifted

1 tsp baking powder

1 tbsp instant coffee

1 tsp hot water

5 tbsp almond milk

TOFFEE NUTS:

50g (2oz) coconut sugar

50g (2oz) honey

50ml (2fl oz) hot water

2 tsp softened butter

75g (3oz) toasted mixed nuts (flaked almonds, walnuts and pecans)

SERVES 6–8

Preheat the oven to 160°C (325°F/gas mark 3). Lightly grease a 23cm (9in) loose-bottomed cake tin and line with parchment paper.

Place the butter, coconut sugar and vanilla extract in a bowl. Using a standalone electric mixer, beat for 8–10 minutes, until light and creamy. Add the egg and egg yolk and beat well, until combined. Add the flour and baking powder and beat again until combined. Place the instant coffee and hot water in a cup and mix well, until the coffee has dissolved. Add the coffee and the almond milk to the butter mixture and fold it through using a large metal spoon. Spoon the mixture into the prepared cake tin.

Bake for 45–50 minutes, until cooked through when tested with a skewer. Leave to cool in the tin for 5 minutes, then transfer to a wire rack and leave to cool completely. When cold, unmold onto a cake stand or plate and set aside.

Meanwhile, to make the toffee nuts, place the coconut sugar, honey and hot water in a small pan over a medium heat. Cook for 6–8 minutes, without stirring, until golden brown and slightly thickened. Add the butter and another tablespoon of hot water. Cook for 3 minutes more, then add the mixed nuts and stir well until they are all evenly coated. Spoon immediately over the cake and serve straight to the table.

Crème Pots with Seasonal Berries

This is just one of the many great puddings that has firm Spanish roots. Very simple to make, it's actually quite light, with all the flavour of the caramel and none of the sticky sweetness. It's similar to the French crème brûlée, except it's not cooked in the oven.

6 egg yolks

150g (5oz) honey

40g (1 ½oz) cornflour

900ml (1 ½ pints) milk

1 cinnamon stick

rind of 1 lemon

rind of 1 orange

2 tbsp Demerara sugar

seasonal berries, such as raspberries, strawberries, blueberries and blackberries, to serve

SERVES 6–8

Place the egg yolks in a heatproof bowl with the honey. Using a hand-held whisk, beat for 5 minutes, until thickened. Tip in the cornflour and mix until well combined.

Place the milk in a small pan with the cinnamon stick, lemon and orange rind. Bring to the boil, then remove from the heat and leave to infuse for 5 minutes.

Strain the milk, discarding the cinnamon stick, lemon and orange rind, then gradually whisk the warm milk into the egg and honey mixture. Place in a clean pan set over a low heat. Cook gently for 10–15 minutes, until the custard coats the back of a wooden spoon. Remove from the heat.

Leave to cool, then pour into individual dishes or ramekins and chill for at least 4 hours (or overnight is best) to allow the custard pots to firm up.

When ready to serve, sprinkle the tops evenly with the Demerara sugar and caramelise with a blow torch or under a preheated hot grill. Arrange on plates with a nice selection of seasonal berries to serve.

Spiced Poached Pears with Crème Fraîche and Toasted Almonds

This delightful dessert will revive even the most jaded palate. The pears improve with keeping, making this an excellent dessert for entertaining. Choose fruit that is perfectly ripe but still quite firm so the flesh doesn't go mushy while you are preparing them.

300ml (½ pint) clear apple juice

juice and finely grated rind of 2 limes

2 whole star anise

1 cinnamon stick, broken in half

½ vanilla pod, split in half

2 tbsp honey

4 firm, ripe pears

2 tbsp toasted flaked almonds

100g (4oz) crème fraîche

SERVES 4

Place the apple juice in a deep-sided pan with a lid (the pan needs to be just large enough to hold the pears in an upright position). Add the lime juice and rind, star anise, cinnamon stick, vanilla pod and honey. Bring to the boil, then reduce the heat and simmer gently for a few minutes to allow the flavours to infuse.

Meanwhile, peel the pears, leaving the stalks attached. Add them to the pan, standing them in an upright position. Cover with the lid and simmer gently for 20–25 minutes, until the pears are tender, basting them from time to time with the liquid. Remove from the heat and leave to cool in the syrup. The cooking time will depend on the ripeness of the pears.

Using a slotted spoon, transfer the pears to a dish and set aside. Reduce the cooking juices by half to a more syrupy consistency. This will take 8–12 minutes. Strain into a jug and leave to cool.

To serve, carefully cut each pear in half so that you don't spoil their beautiful shape. Place the pear halves on a serving platter and drizzle over the spiced syrup. Scatter over the toasted flaked almonds and serve with a separate bowl of crème fraîche.

Index

almond milk, Caramel Pear Tart 230

almonds
  Beef Kofta Curry 110–11
  Lamb Fillet with Blue Cheese and Mint Dressing 125
  Nutty Energy Bites 30
  Spiced Poached Pears with Crème Fraîche and Toasted Almonds 238
  Sticky Orange Upside Down Cake 233
  Three Tomato and Beetroot Salad with Harissa and Goat's Cheese 71

apples
  Apple and Pecan Muffins 215
  Beetroot, Orange, Apple and Pear Juice 5
  Carrot, Ginger, Mint and Orange Juice 2
  Celery, Pear, Apple and Ginger Juice 10
  Fennel, Blueberry, Apple and Lemon Juice 9
  Goat's Cheese, Date and Apple 54

artichoke hearts
  Baked Chicken and Chorizo Rice with Artichokes 95
  Porcini and Artichoke Pasta 137

asparagus
  Cashew Nut Chicken and Asparagus Salad with Mango Salsa 92
  Pancetta Baked Eggs 153

aubergines, Roasted Aubergines with Cherry Tomatoes and Goat's Cheese 134

avocados
  Avocado, Cucumber, Spinach, Kale, Pineapple and Coconut Juice 6
  Crab, Avocado and Mango Salad 68
  Griddled Salmon with Avocado and Sun-Dried Tomatoes 196
  Guacamole 54
  Miso Grilled Hake with Avocado and Lime Salsa 76
  Pulled Chicken Tacos 167
  Quick Quesadillas with Cherry Tomato and Avocado Salsa 223
  Smoked Trout and Prawn Salad with Avocado and Tomato Salsa 173
  Warm Spicy Tiger Prawn Salad 66

bacon
  Butter Bean and Bacon Soup 21
  see also ham; pancetta; pork

Baked Chicken and Chorizo Rice with Artichokes 95

Baked Fish and Chips 160

baking
  Apple and Pecan Muffins 215
  Brown Soda Scones with Walnuts and Flaxseeds 174
  Coconut Carrot Slices 207
  Coffee Cake with Mixed Toffee Nuts 234
  Healthy Anzac Biscuits 226
  Sticky Orange Upside Down Cake 233

bananas
  Hotcakes with Mango and Banana Sauté 212
  Peanut Butter and Banana French Toast Sandwiches 221

beans
  Griddled Halloumi with Red Onion, Haricot Bean and Tomato Salad 143
  Tomato and Red Pepper Broth with Borlotti Beans and Cavolo Nero 190
  see also butter beans; cannellini beans; green beans

beansprouts
  Pad Thai Stir-Fried Noodles with Pork 164–5
  Vietnamese Beef Noodle Soup (Pho Bo) 112

beef
  Beef Kofta Curry 110–11
  Chargrilled Thai Beef Salad 118
  Garlic and Mustard Beef Skewers with Creamy Chive Drizzle 199
  Minute Steaks with White Bean Purée and Sautéed Savoy Cabbage 114–15
  Peppered Beef Burgers with Sweet Potato Wedges 162
  Roast Beef with Dijon and Watercress Wrap 51
  Roast Rolled Rib of Beef with Horseradish Crème Fraîche 116–17
  Vietnamese Beef Noodle Soup (Pho Bo) 112
  Warm Steak Salad with Horseradish Mustard and Balsamic Vinegar 188

beetroot

Beetroot, Orange, Apple and Pear Juice 5

Roasted Beetroot, Feta and Watercress Salad 64

Three Tomato and Beetroot Salad with Harissa and Goat's Cheese 71

Warm Steak Salad with Horseradish Mustard and Balsamic Vinegar 188

berries

Blackberry and Orange Ice Lollies 218

Cinnamon French Toast with Berries and Lime Crème Fraîche 208

Crème Pots with Seasonal Berries 237

Fennel, Blueberry, Apple and Lemon Juice 9

Nutty Energy Bites 30

Watermelon and Raspberry Ice Lollies 218

blue cheese

Lamb Fillet with Blue Cheese and Mint Dressing 125

Pear, Blue Cheese and Spinach Salad with Walnuts 63

bread

Cinnamon French Toast with Berries and Lime Crème Fraîche 208

Peanut Butter and Banana French Toast Sandwiches 221

Tuna and Hummus Bruschetta 26

breadcrumbs

Baked Fish and Chips 160

Cashew Nut Chicken and Asparagus Salad with Mango Salsa 92

Chicken Kiev with Sweet Potato Chips 88–9

One Tray Greek Lamb Mezze 123

Spanish Meatball and Butter Bean Stew 104

Brown Soda Scones with Walnuts and Flaxseeds 174

bulgur wheat

Chicken Tabbouleh Salad with Tahini Drizzle 91

Tabbouleh Salad with Pomegranate and Goat's Cheese 41

butter beans

Butter Bean and Bacon Soup 21

Seared Lamb Fillet with Mediterranean Butter Bean Stew 128

Spanish Meatball and Butter Bean Stew 104

butternut squash, Spice-Crusted Butternut Squash Wedges with Tahini Sauce 34

cabbage

Minute Steaks with White Bean Purée and Sautéed Savoy Cabbage 114–15

Orange and Thyme Pork Steaks with Winter Slaw 99

Smoked Chicken with Asian Slaw 57

Tomato and Red Pepper Broth with Borlotti Beans and Cavolo Nero 190

cannellini beans

Chicken, Shiitake and Cannellini Bean Soup 15

Minute Steaks with White Bean Purée and Sautéed Savoy Cabbage 114–15

capers

Baked Fish and Chips 160

Fresh Tuna Niçoise 74

Grilled Sardines with Salsa Verde 83

Spaghetti with Sardines 177

Tuna and Hummus Bruschetta 26

Caramel Pear Tart 230

carrots

Butter Bean and Bacon Soup 21

Carrot, Ginger, Mint and Orange Juice 2

Coconut Carrot Slices 207

Crunchy Thai Turkey Salad 57

Crunchy Vietnamese Chicken Salad 44–5

Mackerel with Braised Puy Lentils and Sherry Vinaigrette 184

Minestrone Soup with Pesto 18

Roast Rolled Rib of Beef with Horseradish Crème Fraîche 116–17

Root Vegetable, Chicken and Orzo Soup 22

Smoked Chicken with Asian Slaw 57

Spicy Roasted Root Vegetables with Lemon and Herb Couscous 141

Warm Steak Salad with Horseradish Mustard and Balsamic Vinegar 188

cashew nuts

Cashew Nut Chicken and Asparagus Salad with Mango Salsa 92

Chinese Pork and Three Pepper Stir-Fry 107

Fragrant Duck Salad 47

Nutty Energy Bites 30

Spicy Chicken Noodles with Mango 194

cauliflower

Cauliflower and Hazelnut Salad 171

Egg and Cauliflower Curry 146

Pork Goulash with Cauliflower Rice 100

celeriac

Orange and Thyme Pork Steaks with Winter Slaw 99

Warm Steak Salad with Horseradish Mustard and Balsamic Vinegar 188

celery
    Celery, Pear, Apple and Ginger Juice 10
    Minestrone Soup with Pesto 18
    Piquant Tuna Salad 58
    Roast Rolled Rib of Beef with Horseradish Crème Fraîche 116–17
    Root Vegetable, Chicken and Orzo Soup 22
Chargrilled Lamb Chops with Lemon and Herb Quinoa 131
Chargrilled Thai Beef Salad 118
cheese
    Cottage Cheese with Tomato and Cucumber Salsa 57
    Griddled Halloumi with Red Onion, Haricot Bean and Tomato Salad 143
    Ham, Cheese and Pickle 58
    see also blue cheese; feta cheese; goat's cheese; mozzarella; Parmesan cheese
cherry tomatoes
    Chargrilled Thai Beef Salad 118
    Chicken Tabbouleh Salad with Tahini Drizzle 91
    Crab, Avocado and Mango Salad 68
    Crispy Spinach and Feta Filo Pie 138
    Crunchy Vietnamese Chicken Salad 44–5
    Fresh Tuna Niçoise 74
    Griddled Halloumi with Red Onion, Haricot Bean and Tomato Salad 143
    Grilled Sardines with Salsa Verde 83
    Irish Breakfast Omelette 151
    Lamb Fillet with Blue Cheese and Mint Dressing 125
    Miso Grilled Hake with Avocado and Lime Salsa 76
    Moroccan Spiced Lamb Koftas with Chunky Salad and Pitta 126
    One Tray Greek Lamb Mezze 123
    Pulled Chicken Tacos 167
    Quick Quesadillas with Cherry Tomato and Avocado Salsa 223
    Roasted Aubergines with Cherry Tomatoes and Goat's Cheese 134
    Rosemary Roast Lamb Chops with Roasted Potatoes and Cherry Tomatoes 203
    Three Tomato and Beetroot Salad with Harissa and Goat's Cheese 71
chicken
    Baked Chicken and Chorizo Rice with Artichokes 95
    Cashew Nut Chicken and Asparagus Salad with Mango Salsa 92
    Chicken and Coconut Soup 16

Chicken Kiev with Sweet Potato Chips 88–9
Chicken Salad with Cress 53
Chicken, Shiitake and Cannellini Bean Soup 15
Chicken Tabbouleh Salad with Tahini Drizzle 91
Crispy Chicken Strips with Peanut Satay Sauce 224
Crunchy Vietnamese Chicken Salad 44–5
Garlic and Lemon Chicken with Rocket 86
Pulled Chicken Tacos 167
Root Vegetable, Chicken and Orzo Soup 22
Smoked Chicken with Asian Slaw 57
Spicy Chicken Noodles with Mango 194
chickpea flour, Socca Flatbreads 110
chickpeas
    Chicken Tabbouleh Salad with Tahini Drizzle 91
    Red Pepper and Chilli Hummus with Crispy Tortilla Chips 29
    Tuna and Hummus Bruschetta 26
chillies
    Beef Kofta Curry 110–11
    Chargrilled Thai Beef Salad 118
    Chinese Pork and Three Pepper Stir-Fry 107
    Egg and Cauliflower Curry 146
    Pad Thai Stir-Fried Noodles with Pork 164–5
    Sea Bass with Ginger and Chilli 81
    Spicy Roasted Root Vegetables with Lemon and Herb Couscous 141
    Vietnamese Beef Noodle Soup (Pho Bo) 112
Chinese Pork and Three Pepper Stir-Fry 107
chives, Garlic and Mustard Beef Skewers with Creamy Chive Drizzle 199
chorizo, Baked Chicken and Chorizo Rice with Artichokes 95
Cinnamon French Toast with Berries and Lime Crème Fraîche 208
coconut, desiccated
    Coconut Carrot Slices 207
    Healthy Anzac Biscuits 226
    Nutty Energy Bites 30
coconut milk
    Chicken and Coconut Soup 16
    Coconut, Mango and Lemon Rice Pudding 210
    Crispy Chicken Strips with Peanut Satay Sauce 224
    Fragrant Pork and Sweet Potato Thai Red Curry 183
    Satay Prawn Sticks with Griddled Limes 200–1
coconut sugar
    Caramel Pear Tart 230

Coffee Cake with Mixed Toffee Nuts 234

Healthy Anzac Biscuits 226

coconut water, Avocado, Cucumber, Spinach, Kale, Pineapple and Coconut Juice 6

Coffee Cake with Mixed Toffee Nuts 234

Cottage Cheese with Tomato and Cucumber Salsa 57

courgettes

One Tray Greek Lamb Mezze 123

Tomato and Red Pepper Broth with Borlotti Beans and Cavolo Nero 190

Tricolour Quinoa, Mediterranean Vegetable and Mozzarella Salad 38

couscous

Crispy Salmon with Pomegranate and Watercress Couscous 178

Spicy Roasted Root Vegetables with Lemon and Herb Couscous 141

Crab, Avocado and Mango Salad 68

crème fraîche

Cinnamon French Toast with Berries and Lime Crème Fraîche 208

Cumin Roasted Lamb with Pumpkin Mash 187

Lamb Fillet with Blue Cheese and Mint Dressing 125

Pancetta Baked Eggs 153

Roast Rolled Rib of Beef with Horseradish Crème Fraîche 116–17

Smoked Salmon with Horseradish Dressing 53

Smoked Salmon and Watercress Crêpes 154

Smoked Trout and Prawn Salad with Avocado and Tomato Salsa 173

Spiced Poached Pears with Crème Fraîche and Toasted Almonds 238

Tomato and Red Pepper Broth with Borlotti Beans and Cavolo Nero 190

Crème Pots with Seasonal Berries 237

crêpes, Smoked Salmon and Watercress Crêpes 154

cress

Chicken Salad with Cress 53

see also watercress

Crispy Chicken Strips with Peanut Satay Sauce 224

Crispy Salmon with Pomegranate and Watercress Couscous 178

Crispy Spinach and Feta Filo Pie 138

Crunchy Thai Turkey Salad 57

Crunchy Vietnamese Chicken Salad 44–5

cucumbers

Avocado, Cucumber, Spinach, Kale, Pineapple and Coconut Juice 6

Chargrilled Thai Beef Salad 118

Cottage Cheese with Tomato and Cucumber Salsa 57

Crispy Chicken Strips with Peanut Satay Sauce 224

Moroccan Spiced Lamb Koftas with Chunky Salad and Pitta 126

Satay Prawn Sticks with Griddled Limes 200–1

Cumin Roasted Lamb with Pumpkin Mash 187

curry

Beef Kofta Curry 110–11

Egg and Cauliflower Curry 146

Fragrant Pork and Sweet Potato Thai Red Curry 183

dairy free dishes

Garlic and Mustard Beef Skewers with Creamy Chive Drizzle 199

Griddled Salmon with Avocado and Sun-Dried Tomatoes 196

Rosemary Roast Lamb Chops with Roasted Potatoes and Cherry Tomatoes 203

Satay Prawn Sticks with Griddled Limes 200–1

Spicy Chicken Noodles with Mango 194

dates, Goat's Cheese, Date and Apple 54

desserts

Caramel Pear Tart 230

Coconut, Mango and Lemon Rice Pudding 210

Coffee Cake with Mixed Toffee Nuts 234

Crème Pots with Seasonal Berries 237

Hotcakes with Mango and Banana Sauté 212

Spiced Poached Pears with Crème Fraîche and Toasted Almonds 238

Sticky Orange Upside Down Cake 233

dried fruit

Cauliflower and Hazelnut Salad 171

Roasted Beetroot, Feta and Watercress Salad 64

duck, Fragrant Duck Salad 47

eggs

Caramel Pear Tart 230

Cinnamon French Toast with Berries and Lime Crème Fraîche 208

Crispy Chicken Strips with Peanut Satay Sauce 224

Crispy Spinach and Feta Filo Pie 138

Egg and Cauliflower Curry 146

Fresh Tuna Niçoise 74

Ham and Egg Salad Wrap 51

Hotcakes with Mango and Banana Sauté 212

Irish Breakfast Omelette 151

Pad Thai Stir-Fried Noodles with Pork 164–5

Pancetta Baked Eggs 153

Peanut Butter and Banana French Toast Sandwiches 221

Smoked Haddock Hash with Poached Eggs 148–9

Smoked Salmon and Watercress Crêpes 154

fennel

Fennel, Blueberry, Apple and Lemon Juice 9

Minestrone Soup with Pesto 18

Orange and Thyme Pork Steaks with Winter Slaw 99

feta cheese

Crispy Spinach and Feta Filo Pie 138

Moroccan Spiced Lamb Koftas with Chunky Salad and Pitta 126

One Tray Greek Lamb Mezze 123

Roasted Beetroot, Feta and Watercress Salad 64

Seared Lamb Fillet with Mediterranean Butter Bean Stew 128

fish

Sea Bass with Ginger and Chilli 81

Smoked Haddock Hash with Poached Eggs 148–9

Smoked Trout and Prawn Salad with Avocado and Tomato Salsa 173

Spicy Prawn Cakes with Ginger 78

see also hake; mackerel; salmon; sardines; shellfish; tuna

Fragrant Duck Salad 47

Fragrant Pork and Sweet Potato Thai Red Curry 183

Fresh Fruit Ice Lollies 218

Fresh Tuna Niçoise 74

Garlic and Lemon Chicken with Rocket 86

Garlic and Mustard Beef Skewers with Creamy Chive Drizzle 199

ginger

Beef Kofta Curry 110–11

Beetroot, Orange, Apple and Pear Juice 5

Butter Bean and Bacon Soup 21

Carrot, Ginger, Mint and Orange Juice 2

Celery, Pear, Apple and Ginger Juice 10

Chicken and Coconut Soup 16

Chicken, Shiitake and Cannellini Bean Soup 15

Chinese Pork and Three Pepper Stir-Fry 107

Crunchy Vietnamese Chicken Salad 44–5

Fragrant Duck Salad 47

Fragrant Pork and Sweet Potato Thai Red Curry 183

Sea Bass with Ginger and Chilli 81

Spicy Prawn Cakes with Ginger 78

Vietnamese Beef Noodle Soup (Pho Bo) 112

goat's cheese

Goat's Cheese, Date and Apple 54

Roasted Aubergines with Cherry Tomatoes and Goat's Cheese 134

Roasted Red Pepper, Goat's Cheese and Spinach Wrap 51

Tabbouleh Salad with Pomegranate and Goat's Cheese 41

Three Tomato and Beetroot Salad with Harissa and Goat's Cheese 71

Greek yoghurt

Baked Fish and Chips 160

Chicken Tabbouleh Salad with Tahini Drizzle 91

Crispy Salmon with Pomegranate and Watercress Couscous 178

Piquant Tuna Salad 58

green beans

Chinese Pork and Three Pepper Stir-Fry 107

Crunchy Vietnamese Chicken Salad 44–5

Cumin Roasted Lamb with Pumpkin Mash 187

Fresh Tuna Niçoise 74

Garlic and Lemon Chicken with Rocket 86

Lamb Fillet with Blue Cheese and Mint Dressing 125

Minestrone Soup with Pesto 18

Griddled Halloumi with Red Onion, Haricot Bean and Tomato Salad 143

Griddled Salmon with Avocado and Sun-Dried Tomatoes 196

Grilled Sardines with Salsa Verde 83

Guacamole 54

hake

Baked Fish and Chips 160

Miso Grilled Hake with Avocado and Lime Salsa 76

ham

Ham, Cheese and Pickle 58

Ham and Egg Salad Wrap 51

Parma Ham and Tomatoes 54

Parma-Wrapped Pork Fillet with Pesto and Stir-Fried Curly Kale 102–3

see also bacon; pancetta; pork

harissa

Chicken, Shiitake and Cannellini Bean Soup 15

Crispy Salmon with Pomegranate and Watercress Couscous 178

Moroccan Spiced Lamb Koftas with Chunky Salad and Pitta 126

Three Tomato and Beetroot Salad with Harissa and Goat's Cheese 71

hazelnuts

Cauliflower and Hazelnut Salad 171

Spice-Crusted Butternut Squash Wedges with Tahini Sauce 34

Healthy Anzac Biscuits 226

horseradish

Roast Rolled Rib of Beef with Horseradish Crème Fraîche 116–17

Smoked Salmon with Horseradish Dressing 53

Smoked Trout and Prawn Salad with Avocado and Tomato Salsa 173

Warm Steak Salad with Horseradish Mustard and Balsamic Vinegar 188

Hotcakes with Mango and Banana Sauté 212

hummus

Red Pepper and Chilli Hummus with Crispy Tortilla Chips 29

Tuna and Hummus Bruschetta 26

ices, Fresh Fruit Ice Lollies 218

Irish Breakfast Omelette 151

juices

Avocado, Cucumber, Spinach, Kale, Pineapple and Coconut Juice 6

Beetroot, Orange, Apple and Pear Juice 5

Carrot, Ginger, Mint and Orange Juice 2

Celery, Pear, Apple and Ginger Juice 10

Fennel, Blueberry, Apple and Lemon Juice 9

kale

Avocado, Cucumber, Spinach, Kale, Pineapple and Coconut Juice 6

Kale Crisps 33

Parma-Wrapped Pork Fillet with Pesto and Stir-Fried Curly Kale 102–3

kids' favourites

Crispy Chicken Strips with Peanut Satay Sauce 224

Fresh Fruit Ice Lollies 218

Healthy Anzac Biscuits 226

Peanut Butter and Banana French Toast Sandwiches 221

Quick Quesadillas with Cherry Tomato and Avocado Salsa 223

Tropical Mango Ice Lollies 218

lamb

Chargrilled Lamb Chops with Lemon and Herb Quinoa 131

Cumin Roasted Lamb with Pumpkin Mash 187

Lamb Fillet with Blue Cheese and Mint Dressing 125

Moroccan Spiced Lamb Koftas with Chunky Salad and Pitta 126

One Tray Greek Lamb Mezze 123

Rosemary Roast Lamb Chops with Roasted Potatoes and Cherry Tomatoes 203

Seared Lamb Fillet with Mediterranean Butter Bean Stew 128

lemongrass

Chicken and Coconut Soup 16

Satay Prawn Sticks with Griddled Limes 200–1

Warm Spicy Tiger Prawn Salad 66

lemons

Baked Fish and Chips 160

Celery, Pear, Apple and Ginger Juice 10

Chargrilled Lamb Chops with Lemon and Herb Quinoa 131

Coconut, Mango and Lemon Rice Pudding 210

Crab, Avocado and Mango Salad 68

Crème Pots with Seasonal Berries 237

Crispy Salmon with Pomegranate and Watercress Couscous 178

Fennel, Blueberry, Apple and Lemon Juice 9

Garlic and Lemon Chicken with Rocket 86

Griddled Halloumi with Red Onion, Haricot Beand and Tomato Salad 143

Griddled Salmon with Avocado and Sun-Dried Tomatoes 196

Porcini and Artichoke Pasta 137

Red Pepper and Chilli Hummus with Crispy Tortilla Chips 29

Smoked Salmon and Watercress Crêpes 154

Spicy Roasted Root Vegetables with Lemon and Herb Couscous 141

Tabbouleh Salad with Pomegranate and Goat's Cheese 41

Tricolour Quinoa, Mediterranean Vegetable and Mozzarella Salad 38

Tuna and Hummus Bruschetta 26

lentils, Mackerel with Braised Puy Lentils and Sherry Vinaigrette 184

lettuce

Cashew Nut Chicken and Asparagus Salad with Mango Salsa 92

Cottage Cheese with Tomato and Cucumber Salsa 57

Crab, Avocado and Mango Salad 68

Crunchy Thai Turkey Salad 57

Fragrant Duck Salad 47

Fresh Tuna Niçoise 74

Moroccan Spiced Lamb Koftas with Chunky Salad and Pitta 126

Smoked Chicken with Asian Slaw 57

Tabbouleh Salad with Pomegranate and Goat's Cheese 41

limes

Avocado, Cucumber, Spinach, Kale, Pineapple and Coconut Juice 6

Cinnamon French Toast with Berries and Lime Crème Fraîche 208

Miso Grilled Hake with Avocado and Lime Salsa 76

Satay Prawn Sticks with Griddled Limes 200-1

Spiced Poached Pears with Crème Fraîche and Toasted Almonds 238

Tropical Mango Ice Lollies 218

lunchboxes

Chicken Salad with Cress 53

Cottage Cheese with Tomato and Cucumber Salsa 57

Crunchy Thai Turkey Salad 57

Goat's Cheese, Date and Apple 54

Guacamole 54

Ham, Cheese and Pickle 58

Ham and Egg Salad Wrap 51

Mackerel Pâté with Watercress 53

Parma Ham and Tomatoes 54

Piquant Tuna Salad 58

Prawn, Tomato and Rocket 58

Roast Beef with Dijon and Watercress Wrap 51

Roasted Red Pepper, Goat's Cheese and Spinach Wrap 51

Smoked Chicken with Asian Slaw 57

Smoked Salmon with Horseradish Dressing 53

lunches (low-carb)

Crunchy Vietnamese Chicken Salad 44-5

Fragrant Duck Salad 47

Roasted Red Pepper and Walnut Dip with Crudités 43

Tabbouleh Salad with Pomegranate and Goat's Cheese 41

Tricolour Quinoa, Mediterranean Vegetable and Mozzarella Salad 38

mackerel

Mackerel with Braised Puy Lentils and Sherry Vinaigrette 184

Mackerel Pâté with Watercress 53

mangos

Cashew Nut Chicken and Asparagus Salad with Mango Salsa 92

Coconut, Mango and Lemon Rice Pudding 210

Crab, Avocado and Mango Salad 68

Fragrant Duck Salad 47

Hotcakes with Mango and Banana Sauté 212

Spicy Chicken Noodles with Mango 194

Tropical Mango Ice Lollies 218

Warm Spicy Tiger Prawn Salad 66

Minestrone Soup with Pesto 18

mint

Carrot, Ginger, Mint and Orange Juice 2

Chicken Tabbouleh Salad with Tahini Drizzle 91

Minute Steaks with White Bean Purée and Sautéed Savoy Cabbage 114-15

Miso Grilled Hake with Avocado and Lime Salsa 76

Moroccan Spiced Lamb Koftas with Chunky Salad and Pitta 126

mozzarella

Quick Quesadillas with Cherry Tomato and Avocado Salsa 223

Tricolour Quinoa, Mediterranean Vegetable and Mozzarella Salad 38

mushrooms

Chicken, Shiitake and Cannellini Bean Soup 15

Irish Breakfast Omelette 151

Lamb Fillet with Blue Cheese and Mint Dressing 125

Porcini and Artichoke Pasta 137

noodles

Chicken and Coconut Soup 16

Pad Thai Stir-Fried Noodles with Pork 164–5

Spicy Chicken Noodles with Mango 194

Vietnamese Beef Noodle Soup (Pho Bo) 112

nuts

Apple and Pecan Muffins 215

Coffee Cake with Mixed Toffee Nuts 234

Nutty Energy Bites 30

see also almonds; cashew nuts; hazelnuts; peanuts; pine nuts; walnuts

olives

Fresh Tuna Niçoise 74

Griddled Halloumi with Red Onion, Haricot Bean and Tomato Salad 143

Grilled Sardines with Salsa Verde 83

Moroccan Spiced Lamb Koftas with Chunky Salad and Pitta 126

One Tray Greek Lamb Mezze 123

Spaghetti with Sardines 177

Tapenade 74

Tricolour Quinoa, Mediterranean Vegetable and Mozzarella Salad 38

Omega-3

Brown Soda Scones with Walnuts and Flaxseeds 174

Cauliflower and Hazelnut Salad 171

Crispy Salmon with Pomegranate and Watercress Couscous 178

Mackerel with Braised Puy Lentils and Sherry Vinaigrette 184

Smoked Trout and Prawn Salad with Avocado and Tomato Salsa 173

Spaghetti with Sardines 177

One Tray Greek Lamb Mezze 123

onions

Beef Kofta Curry 110–11

Mackerel with Braised Puy Lentils and Sherry Vinaigrette 184

Minute Steaks with White Bean Purée and Sautéed Savoy Cabbage 114–15

Porcini and Artichoke Pasta 137

Pork Goulash with Cauliflower Rice 100

Roast Rolled Rib of Beef with Horseradish Crème Fraîche 116–17

Smoked Haddock Hash with Poached Eggs 148–9

see also red onions; shallots; spring onions

oranges

Beetroot, Orange, Apple and Pear Juice 5

Blackberry and Orange Ice Lollies 218

Carrot, Ginger, Mint and Orange Juice 2

Crème Pots with Seasonal Berries 237

Orange and Thyme Pork Steaks with Winter Slaw 99

Sticky Orange Upside Down Cake 233

Pad Thai Stir-Fried Noodles with Pork 164–5

pancetta

Irish Breakfast Omelette 151

Pancetta Baked Eggs 153

Tomato and Red Pepper Broth with Borlotti Beans and Cavolo Nero 190

see also bacon; ham; pork

Parma Ham and Tomatoes 54

Parma-Wrapped Pork Fillet with Pesto and Stir-Fried Curly Kale 102–3

Parmesan cheese

Crispy Spinach and Feta Filo Pie 138

Pancetta Baked Eggs 153

Porcini and Artichoke Pasta 137

parsnips, Spicy Roasted Root Vegetables with Lemon and Herb Couscous 141

pasta

Minestrone Soup with Pesto 18

Porcini and Artichoke Pasta 137

Root Vegetable, Chicken and Orzo Soup 22

Spaghetti with Sardines 177

pâté, Mackerel Pâté with Watercress 53

peanut butter

Crispy Chicken Strips with Peanut Satay Sauce 224

Nutty Energy Bites 30

Peanut Butter and Banana French Toast Sandwiches 221

peanuts

Crunchy Thai Turkey Salad 57

Pad Thai Stir-Fried Noodles with Pork 164–5

Satay Prawn Sticks with Griddled Limes 200–1

pears
  Beetroot, Orange, Apple and Pear Juice 5
  Caramel Pear Tart 230
  Celery, Pear, Apple and Ginger Juice 10
  Pear, Blue Cheese and Spinach Salad with Walnuts 63
  Spiced Poached Pears with Crème Fraîche and Toasted Almonds 238
Peppered Beef Burgers with Sweet Potato Wedges 162
peppers
  Chicken Tabbouleh Salad with Tahini Drizzle 91
  Chinese Pork and Three Pepper Stir-Fry 107
  Pork Goulash with Cauliflower Rice 100
  Quick Quesadillas with Cherry Tomato and Avocado Salsa 223
  Red Pepper and Chilli Hummus with Crispy Tortilla Chips 29
  Roasted Red Pepper, Goat's Cheese and Spinach Wrap 51
  Roasted Red Pepper and Walnut Dip with Crudités 43
  Spanish Meatball and Butter Bean Stew 104
  Tomato and Red Pepper Broth with Borlotti Beans and Cavolo Nero 190
  Tricolour Quinoa, Mediterranean Vegetable and Mozzarella Salad 38
pesto
  Parma-Wrapped Pork Fillet with Pesto and Stir-Fried Curly Kale 102–3
  Tomato and Red Pepper Broth with Borlotti Beans and Cavolo Nero 190
pickle, Ham, Cheese and Pickle 58
pine nuts
  Parma-Wrapped Pork Fillet with Pesto and Stir-Fried Curly Kale 102–3
  Roasted Beetroot, Feta and Watercress Salad 64
pineapples, Avocado, Cucumber, Spinach, Kale, Pineapple and Coconut Juice 6
Piquant Tuna Salad 58
pomegranates
  Crispy Salmon with Pomegranate and Watercress Couscous 178
  Tabbouleh Salad with Pomegranate and Goat's Cheese 41
Porcini and Artichoke Pasta 137
pork
  Chinese Pork and Three Pepper Stir-Fry 107
  Fragrant Pork and Sweet Potato Thai Red Curry 183
  Orange and Thyme Pork Steaks with Winter Slaw 99

Pad Thai Stir-Fried Noodles with Pork 164–5
Parma-Wrapped Pork Fillet with Pesto and Stir-Fried Curly Kale 102–3
Pork Goulash with Cauliflower Rice 100
Spanish Meatball and Butter Bean Stew 104
see also bacon; ham; pancetta
potatoes
  Baked Fish and Chips 160
  Cumin Roasted Lamb with Pumpkin Mash 187
  Fresh Tuna Niçoise 74
  One Tray Greek Lamb Mezze 123
  Rosemary Roast Lamb Chops with Roasted Potatoes and Cherry Tomatoes 203
  Smoked Haddock Hash with Poached Eggs 148–9
Prawn, Tomato and Rocket 58
Pulled Chicken Tacos 167
pumpkin, Cumin Roasted Lamb with Pumpkin Mash 187

Quick Quesadillas with Cherry Tomato and Avocado Salsa 223
quinoa
  Chargrilled Lamb Chops with Lemon and Herb Quinoa 131
  Tricolour Quinoa, Mediterranean Vegetable and Mozzarella Salad 38

red onions
  Cashew Nut Chicken and Asparagus Salad with Mango Salsa 92
  Cauliflower and Hazelnut Salad 171
  Chicken Tabbouleh Salad with Tahini Drizzle 91
  Griddled Halloumi with Red Onion, Haricot Bean and Tomato Salad 143
  Moroccan Spiced Lamb Koftas with Chunky Salad and Pitta 126
  One Tray Greek Lamb Mezze 123
  Peppered Beef Burgers with Sweet Potato Wedges 162
  Seared Lamb Fillet with Mediterranean Butter Bean Stew 128
  Spaghetti with Sardines 177
  Spanish Meatball and Butter Bean Stew 104
  Spicy Chicken Noodles with Mango 194
  Spicy Roasted Root Vegetables with Lemon and Herb Couscous 141

Tricolour Quinoa, Mediterranean Vegetable and Mozzarella Salad 38

Red Pepper and Chilli Hummus with Crispy Tortilla Chips 29

rice

Baked Chicken and Chorizo Rice with Artichokes 95

Coconut, Mango and Lemon Rice Pudding 210

Seafood Paella 159

Roast Beef with Dijon and Watercress Wrap 51

Roast Rolled Rib of Beef with Horseradish Crème Fraîche 116–17

Roasted Aubergines with Cherry Tomatoes and Goat's Cheese 134

Roasted Beetroot, Feta and Watercress Salad 64

Roasted Red Pepper, Goat's Cheese and Spinach Wrap 51

Roasted Red Pepper and Walnut Dip with Crudités 43

rocket

Garlic and Lemon Chicken with Rocket 86

Prawn, Tomato and Rocket 58

Root Vegetable, Chicken and Orzo Soup 22

Rosemary Roast Lamb Chops with Roasted Potatoes and Cherry Tomatoes 203

salads

Cashew Nut Chicken and Asparagus Salad with Mango Salsa 92

Cauliflower and Hazelnut Salad 171

Chargrilled Thai Beef Salad 118

Chicken Tabbouleh Salad with Tahini Drizzle 91

Cottage Cheese with Tomato and Cucumber Salsa 57

Crab, Avocado and Mango Salad 68

Crunchy Thai Turkey Salad 57

Crunchy Vietnamese Chicken Salad 44–5

Fragrant Duck Salad 47

Fresh Tuna Niçoise 74

Griddled Halloumi with Red Onion, Haricot Bean and Tomato Salad 143

Lamb Fillet with Blue Cheese and Mint Dressing 125

Moroccan Spiced Lamb Koftas with Chunky Salad and Pitta 126

Pear, Blue Cheese and Spinach Salad with Walnuts 63

Piquant Tuna Salad 58

Prawn, Tomato and Rocket 58

Roasted Beetroot, Feta and Watercress Salad 64

Roasted Red Pepper and Walnut Dip with Crudités 43

Smoked Chicken with Asian Slaw 57

Smoked Trout and Prawn Salad with Avocado and Tomato Salsa 173

Tabbouleh Salad with Pomegranate and Goat's Cheese 41

Three Tomato and Beetroot Salad with Harissa and Goat's Cheese 71

Tricolour Quinoa, Mediterranean Vegetable and Mozzarella Salad 38

Warm Spicy Tiger Prawn Salad 66

Warm Steak Salad with Horseradish Mustard and Balsamic Vinegar 188

salmon

Crispy Salmon with Pomegranate and Watercress Couscous 178

Griddled Salmon with Avocado and Sun-Dried Tomatoes 196

Smoked Salmon with Horseradish Dressing 53

Smoked Salmon and Watercress Crêpes 154

sardines

Grilled Sardines with Salsa Verde 83

Spaghetti with Sardines 177

Satay Prawn Sticks with Griddled Limes 200–1

Sea Bass with Ginger and Chilli 81

Seafood Paella 159

Seared Lamb Fillet with Mediterranean Butter Bean Stew 128

seeds

Baked Fish and Chips 160

Brown Soda Scones with Walnuts and Flaxseeds 174

Chinese Pork and Three Pepper Stir-Fry 107

Crispy Salmon with Pomegranate and Watercress Couscous 178

Nutty Energy Bites 30

Spice-Crusted Butternut Squash Wedges with Tahini Sauce 34

Spicy Prawn Cakes with Ginger 78

Spicy Roasted Root Vegetables with Lemon and Herb Couscous 141

shallots

Chargrilled Thai Beef Salad 118

Crunchy Vietnamese Chicken Salad 44

Garlic and Lemon Chicken with Rocket 86

Pad Thai Stir-Fried Noodles with Pork 164–5

Roasted Aubergines with Cherry Tomatoes and Goat's Cheese 134

Warm Spicy Tiger Prawn Salad 66

shellfish
  Crab, Avocado and Mango Salad 68
  Prawn, Tomato and Rocket 58
  Satay Prawn Sticks with Griddled Limes 200–1
  Seafood Paella 159
  Smoked Trout and Prawn Salad with Avocado and Tomato Salsa 173
  Spicy Prawn Cakes with Ginger 78
  Warm Spicy Tiger Prawn Salad 66
Smoked Chicken with Asian Slaw 57
Smoked Haddock Hash with Poached Eggs 148–9
Smoked Salmon with Horseradish Dressing 53
Smoked Salmon and Watercress Crêpes 154
Smoked Trout and Prawn Salad with Avocado and Tomato Salsa 173
snacks
  Kale Crisps 33
  Nutty Energy Bites 30
  Red Pepper and Chilli Hummus with Crispy Tortilla Chips 29
  Spice-Crusted Butternut Squash Wedges with Tahini Sauce 34
  Tuna and Hummus Bruschetta 26
soups
  Butter Bean and Bacon Soup 21
  Chicken and Coconut Soup 16
  Chicken, Shiitake and Cannellini Bean Soup 15
  Minestrone Soup with Pesto 18
  Root Vegetable, Chicken and Orzo Soup 22
  Tomato and Red Pepper Broth with Borlotti Beans and Cavolo Nero 190
  Vietnamese Beef Noodle Soup (Pho Bo) 112
soya yoghurt, Garlic and Mustard Beef Skewers with Creamy Chive Drizzle 199
Spaghetti with Sardines 177
Spanish Meatball and Butter Bean Stew 104
spelt flour, Healthy Anzac Biscuits 226
Spice-Crusted Butternut Squash Wedges with Tahini Sauce 34
Spiced Poached Pears with Crème Fraîche and Toasted Almonds 238
Spicy Chicken Noodles with Mango 194
Spicy Prawn Cakes with Ginger 78
Spicy Roasted Root Vegetables with Lemon and Herb Couscous 141
spinach
  Avocado, Cucumber, Spinach, Kale, Pineapple and Coconut Juice 6

Baked Chicken and Chorizo Rice with Artichokes 95
Cauliflower and Hazelnut Salad 171
Chicken Kiev with Sweet Potato Chips 88–9
Crispy Spinach and Feta Filo Pie 138
Irish Breakfast Omelette 151
Pear, Blue Cheese and Spinach Salad with Walnuts 63
Roasted Red Pepper, Goat's Cheese and Spinach Wrap 51
spring onions
  Chargrilled Lamb Chops with Lemon and Herb Quinoa 131
  Chargrilled Thai Beef Salad 118
  Crispy Spinach and Feta Filo Pie 138
  Fragrant Duck Salad 47
  Fragrant Pork and Sweet Potato Thai Red Curry 183
  Irish Breakfast Omelette 151
  Pad Thai Stir-Fried Noodles with Pork 164–5
  Quick Quesadillas with Cherry Tomato and Avocado Salsa 223
  Sea Bass with Ginger and Chilli 81
  Vietnamese Beef Noodle Soup (Pho Bo) 112
  Warm Spicy Tiger Prawn Salad 66
Sticky Orange Upside Down Cake 233
sugar free
  Apple and Pecan Muffins 215
  Cinnamon French Toast with Berries and Lime Crème Fraîche 208
  Coconut Carrot Slices 207
  Coconut, Mango and Lemon Rice Pudding 210
  Hotcakes with Mango and Banana Sauté 212
sweet potatoes
  Chicken Kiev with Sweet Potato Chips 88–9
  Fragrant Pork and Sweet Potato Thai Red Curry 183
  Peppered Beef Burgers with Sweet Potato Wedges 162

Tabbouleh Salad with Pomegranate and Goat's Cheese 41
tahini
  Chicken Tabbouleh Salad with Tahini Drizzle 91
  Spice-Crusted Butternut Squash Wedges with Tahini Sauce 34
takeaways
  Baked Fish and Chips 160
  Pad Thai Stir-Fried Noodles with Pork 164–5

Peppered Beef Burgers with Sweet Potato Wedges 162

Pulled Chicken Tacos 167

Seafood Paella 159

Three Tomato and Beetroot Salad with Harissa and Goat's Cheese 71

tomatoes

Cottage Cheese with Tomato and Cucumber Salsa 57

Parma Ham and Tomatoes 54

Peppered Beef Burgers with Sweet Potato Wedges 162

Prawn, Tomato and Rocket 58

Seafood Paella 159

Smoked Trout and Prawn Salad with Avocado and Tomato Salsa 173

Tabbouleh Salad with Pomegranate and Goat's Cheese 41

Tomato and Red Pepper Broth with Borlotti Beans and Cavolo Nero 190

see also cherry tomatoes

tomatoes, sieved

Beef Kofta Curry 110–11

Pulled Chicken Tacos 167

tomatoes, sun-dried

Griddled Salmon with Avocado and Sun-Dried Tomatoes 196

Pancetta Baked Eggs 153

Roasted Red Pepper and Walnut Dip with Crudités 43

tomatoes, tinned

Egg and Cauliflower Curry 146

Pork Goulash with Cauliflower Rice 100

Seared Lamb Fillet with Mediterranean Butter Bean Stew 128

Spaghetti with Sardines 177

Spanish Meatball and Butter Bean Stew 104

Tricolour Quinoa, Mediterranean Vegetable and Mozzarella Salad 38

Tropical Mango Ice Lollies 218

tuna

Fresh Tuna Niçoise 74

Piquant Tuna Salad 58

Tuna and Hummus Bruschetta 26

turkey, Crunchy Thai Turkey Salad 57

vegetarian dishes

Crispy Spinach and Feta Filo Pie 138

Egg and Cauliflower Curry 146

Griddled Halloumi with Red Onion, Haricot Bean and Tomato Salad 143

Porcini and Artichoke Pasta 137

Roasted Aubergines with Cherry Tomatoes and Goat's Cheese 134

Spicy Roasted Root Vegetables with Lemon and Herb Couscous 141

Vietnamese Beef Noodle Soup (Pho Bo) 112

walnuts

Brown Soda Scones with Walnuts and Flaxseeds 174

Pear, Blue Cheese and Spinach Salad with Walnuts 63

Roasted Red Pepper and Walnut Dip with Crudités 43

Warm Spicy Tiger Prawn Salad 66

Warm Steak Salad with Horseradish Mustard and Balsamic Vinegar 188

watercress

Crispy Salmon with Pomegranate and Watercress Couscous 178

Mackerel Pâté with Watercress 53

Roast Beef with Dijon and Watercress Wrap 51

Roasted Beetroot, Feta and Watercress Salad 64

Smoked Salmon and Watercress Crêpes 154

Warm Spicy Tiger Prawn Salad 66

Watermelon and Raspberry Ice Lollies 218

wheat free dishes

Cumin Roasted Lamb with Pumpkin Mash 187

Fragrant Pork and Sweet Potato Thai Red Curry 183

Mackerel with Braised Puy Lentils and Sherry Vinaigrette 184

Tomato and Red Pepper Broth with Borlotti Beans and Cavolo Nero 190

Warm Steak Salad with Horseradish Mustard and Balsamic Vinegar 188

wraps

Ham and Egg Salad 51

Quick Quesadillas with Cherry Tomato and Avocado Salsa 223

Roast Beef with Dijon and Watercress 51

Roasted Red Pepper, Goat's Cheese and Spinach 51